AIR UNPLUGGED

AIR UNPLUGGED

OLGA K. AKOPIANTS

NEW DEGREE PRESS

COPYRIGHT © 2021 OLGA K. AKOPIANTS

All rights reserved.

AIR UNPLUGGED

ISBN 978-1-63730-421-1 *Paperback*
      978-1-63730-499-0 *Kindle Ebook*
      978-1-63730-500-3 *Ebook*

CONTENTS

AUTHOR'S NOTE

If you know me personally, you might characterize me as a neurotic person. We all like to speculate on "what could have happened" or ask "what if?" We reimagine the past, but we also fantasize about the future. It's an innate human quality.

Having freshly experienced a near-death car accident, I became an anxious driver. Ironically, I picked up an EMT job in which half of the job was driving a gigantic ambulance. Your chances of smashing side mirrors increase by 50 percent when driving such vehicle. To make matters worse, these trucks had concerning issues with overheating engines, broken air conditioning, or busted turbo pipes. Imagine the world's slowest ambulance, which can hardly kick into second gear and hit twenty-five miles per hour, responding with lights and sirens to an emergency. Or the heart-clenching feeling when the brakes of your heavy Ford truck stop braking on a hilly terrain city. Over the period of a month, the ambulances broke down in the middle of nowhere with transported COVID-19 patients to others having a diabetic emergency. And on top of that, sprinkle the typical burnout from understaffing, sexism from patients, and workplace drama.

My fear made me wonder what would happen if I ended up in an accident while in this junk truck?

It set me down a trail of speculation. What if I became stranded in the wild? What is it like to truly live in the wild? If I were put into such an extreme situation without phone service or other functional technology, would I be able to survive? Being in the wild is the perfect place to test whether someone has the right inner mindset to make it out alive with only their willpower. As a result, this book tests the protagonist with the question, "With nothing else but your willpower, are you made of the right stuff to survive?"

A significant portion of this book was written during the COVID-19 lockdown that left no one unscathed. People lost jobs or felt the brunt of loneliness, and loved ones died. The pandemic is a peak example of how events and our environment are beyond our control. However, what we are able to control are our own reactions to failures and tragedy. Surviving the worst-case scenario is possible if one practices stoic-like grit. In fact, part of my research for *Air Unplugged* involved reading classic stoic meditations, which inspired character's inner philosophies.

Even during writing, I faced a lot of rejections. I was hyper-critical of my own writing because I was scared to write something unworthy and felt imposter syndrome. Marketing was a whole different beast because that involves being confident and bold—which I can be if there's a good basis to be confident. When it came to marketing, I explored a lot of avenues only to meet dead ends. I wanted to stop the project many times, but I also knew that if I didn't continue, *Air Unplugged* would sit as a huge file on my drive folder. What seemed impossible became a reality.

Traditionally, the most popular survival stories (*The Martian*, *Hatchet*) have included male protagonists; however, grit and perseverance are not only masculine traits. I wanted to include a protagonist with feminine traits who demonstrates grit and a stubbornness to live. This is not for the sake of politics, but a demonstration to show that anyone—myself, yourself—can push through the obstacles that life throws at us.

Everyone is fighting their own battle, and I hope that you take a break and cheer Ary on as she fights her own battles.

CHAPTER 1

HUMAN AFTER ALL

I know they're going to say I'm lying, but I swear on my late mother's uploaded consciousness that I will only tell the truth.

Mother's funeral included a generation's worth of drama against a blurry background of grief. The aunty with the outdated, poufed hair yelled at me for burying her with the traditional option. This wasn't my choice; it was just my mother's wish to be buried just like her mother and her mother's mother. My teenage nephews shuffled their feet as they apologized for my loss, bending to the will of their mother. Mom's sleazy ex-husband nonchalantly brought up her will at least five times within a ten-minute conversation.

Your mother would have laughed at how little he pretends to care about that will, Cort thought to me as mother's ex-husband walked away from us before hearing more.

I couldn't disagree with her. They say that friendly robo-assistants like Cort (Cort is a virtual assistant operating through a set of earbuds who has access to its owner's thoughts) don't understand human emotions, but more often than not, Cort proves that general opinion wrong.

Mother, before she had declined, had the spunk of an impulsive teenager. She ran robotic repair businesses, sold them off, then started the cycle again. Although I always attacked her with criticism, her death made me admire her rash decisions. She loved to risk and gamble all throughout her life, and I had been a doubting fool.

"It was all coming along anyway," a cousin whispered nearby. My chest tightened and heat rose through my cheeks. They blamed my mother, but they didn't understand her.

Mother's condition had deteriorated for two prolonged years after she had ultimately refused medications to keep her mind intact. And so she declined into the body of a titan with the mind of a two-year-old. I became her primary caretaker: I cleaned her soiled bed sheets from waste, fed her bland food, and bought her miscellaneous tools to help her daily function despite her tremors. Some days were easy, and she'd say funny phrases while walking in my one-thousand-square-foot condo.

"Golly, this place is spacious!" She'd say and stretch by the window overlooking New Khan City (NK City).

Other times, she would fail to recognize that I was her daughter.

"Get me out of here!" Mother would scream at me in a tone I had never known before her dementia. Her fits were always disturbing, and I used to crouch away in self-defense when she had them. Once I had accepted that she would have these tantrums, I would leave the apartment for fresh air and converse with Cort about something different.

Another aunty poked my shoulder, interrupting my thoughts.

"You poor doll! So sad that your mother didn't get to see you start your dream job!" Aunty told me.

"It is poor timing." I flinched away from the touch. "I'll be starting very soon."

"You're still going back to work? Oh dear. You should take a shuttle to the beach down south." Aunty cooed. "That's how I got over my husband's death. I was sulking for months but my girlfriends shook me out of it."

"I'll consider it," I smiled with reassurance, but my mind had already taken a shuttle on how I could escape with the social vortex. The social vortex was a comforting space, full of dazzling images and a billion years' worth of entertainment. It was pure ecstasy, like cotton candy wrapped in glitter.

Despite my distractions, I still couldn't make sense of her death. I talked with Cort, my only friend, to try make sense of it. To me, Mother's death was as expected but also a random drop in the bucket. Life would not be the same again because I had lost my first best friend ever—my caretaker—and gained a peculiar child to take care of.

Cort became my second best friend when she was introduced in her tiny pearl case at three years old. She was meant to be a safety measure so my mom knew my whereabouts as she worked. Having a Cort was a normal part of our society. While previous generations had feared letting their children outside, a Cort's presence provided a special reassurance about child safety. Gradually, Cort began to play a heavier role in my upbringing, tutoring, and life management.

Together, we remembered how proud my mom was when she had closed her first business deal. That day, she celebrated by inviting her girlfriends and baking the most delicious whipped cream cake speckled with strawberries. I remembered that I was more than disappointed when we had to leave our old home in New Jochi, but mother's determination and positivity was infectious.

Throughout the time that I shut myself away to grieve, I interacted with no one other than Cort. As she had done most of my life, she helped me manage my time and counted down the days when I would need to snap out of the daze to once again start fresh. I was about to start my twelfth job that I have had over the course of five years of juggling being a caretaker, student, and employee.

~

A week later, I awoke to a cold dawn, with the early white rays of hazy sunlight hitting my covers. I stared at the ceiling, unmoving, waiting for the dreadful alarm to sound. On some floor below, a morning alarm had already sung its jolly song, leaving me to anticipate my own alarm's ring. Not that I was planning to stop it from happening. I decided to start my day without it.

The warmth of the heated toilet and the chill of the tiled bathroom floor caused a spiral of discomfort to shoot through my body, starting at my toes and leaving a trail of goosebumps.

"Do I look like a trustworthy flight nurse in this suit?" I turned around in the mirror to see the tightness around my scapulothoracic joints. Even if my mom were here in a demented state, she would have rained encouragement on me unprompted.

Sure, you look splendid, Cort told me. I rinsed the caky sleep out of my eyes. "You must be tired. Don't worry, you'll do well even if it's the first day."

"I was awake before the alarm went off." I rummaged through my makeup bag to find an eye bag concealer. "Hope coffee doesn't make my hands shake too much for starting IV lines."

I recommend the lighter green tone, Cort said. *I can get started on your SeroSoothe and caffeine tablet orders.* I carried on with her suggestion.

"Guess you're right," I murmured to her. There was a remarkable difference between both of my eyes, with the now improved left one and the bloodshot *I-am-an-insomniac* right one.

You'll be great Ary, Cort assured me. *It's unfortunate how much poor luck has been following you. By the way, it would be a good idea to leave right now to catch the 6:15 shuttle.*

"Thank you Cort," I said, tying up the thick shoelaces of my boots. "That funeral was everything I had dreaded but exactly what you predicted. I couldn't have been more alone in that situation."

I'm sorry to hear you have felt estranged from almost everyone. I'm here to help you through this period, but do understand that I can't last forever for your sake. I'm not human, after all.

I gingerly carried my earbud pearls to their charging port.

"Ah, that feels better." Court said on her loudspeaker. That was Cort's way of saying she's charging while I stepped outside with my usual caution.

The outside air was cold in contrast to the sweltering heat of yesterday. Despite the frigid weather, there was plenty of energy and movement in the streets. Buzzing from incoming shuttles, billboard lights, and people murmuring into their earphones were muddled in the open air. The yellow-white city lights beamed at me as I speed walked past the other early-bird workers.

There was a stench of sulfur from an alleyway. A high schooler passed me on her hoverboard. That had been me just ten years ago. I wound my jacket more tightly around my body, shielding myself from the incoming tunnel wind.

As I was approaching the shuttle stop to take a shuttle to NK Hospital district, my eyes were caught by a billboard in parallel with apartment buildings. It displayed a tan brunette with the perfect smile while leaning back as a handsome, well-built man smiled at her with a gallant expression, offering her the keycard to his vehicle. "REALIZE YOUR BEST LIFE. BE WITH SOMEONE WHO MATCHES YOU 100 PERCENT ONLY." And a subtitle, *"Apply to be matched via our best data predicting records!"*

What a foreign idea. Prior to my mother's decline, of course dating was a concern of mine. That idea had been worn out like a tossed river pebble and the concern became to sustain my demented mother and myself. Now, I was trying out a career path that I had worked the graveyard shift on to get the proper education.

There was a significant pressure within me to like the career of a flight nurse because this was the first decision that I was selfishly making for myself.

As the early shuttle rolled to a pause, I let it sweep me away toward the reality of the NK hospital district.

CHAPTER 2

SALMON AND SNAKES

Hospitals were different many years ago. Small clinics sprouted from the religious passions of well-intentioned people. My nursing textbooks had black-and-white photos showing stretched hallways with streaming sunlight and nurses in immaculate aprons angled over patients. The paradox concerning antiquated medicine was that, for one's survival, the patient would have lived longer had they stayed at home to their wife's continuous prayers or a burning candle.

What has stayed the same, though, is that no matter the hour, the hospital is a lively beehive. The hallways are bustling with nurses, administrators, various aids, robots tugging supplies, a variety of therapists, doctors, and visitors. Even with the high energy and a multitude of colorful scrubs darting around, there are only a few windows and ceiling lights, causing even the healthy to look frightfully sick.

The shuttle rolled Cort and me into the hospital district, a collection of buzzing skyscrapers and neon lights painted against the cool mint of the morning ice. Under normal conditions, I would have been more excited about starting fresh. But as I stepped off the shuttle, I was reluctant to rush with the wave. And as Cort guided me toward the correct street, I was reluctant to pick up my feet. Sensing my melancholy,

Cort even played a pick-me-up playlist while guiding me into the main atrium of the NK hospital. My eyes glazed over the map directory, struggling to concentrate on the department title that I needed.

It seems like you're in a caloric deficit. Cort murmured in my ear something about eating food, which I wanted to ignore.

And yet, an intoxicating, beautiful smell of breakfast curled into my nose. Smoked breakfast meat topped with rich tomato sauce and spicy pickles sandwiched between enriched sweet bread.

Do I have enough time? I shouldn't be late. I thought to Cort, bumping into a robot that decided to stop its preprogrammed routine in the middle of the hallway. I got some angry looks from passersby. It didn't matter, because a red-yellow glittering light was beckoning me to come, the smell's arms pulling me into a tight hug.

There's plenty of time and you should take care of your needs. Cort said as I approached the register.

"Welcome to Che's," a jovial automated cashier called out to me. "How can I serve you today?"

I ordered a classic breakfast CLP with cheese and bagel. I knew that I didn't need anything else, but after scanning the rest of the screen, my eyes were drawn to a figure of a golden roasted salmon. (CLP, short for Chicken Lamb Pork Inc., was a company that created the most well-known meat substitute that would eventually replace morally questionable meat products.)

Look at that salmon. Your mom's favorite food. Cort recalled. *That was one of the main dishes at her sixtieth birthday party. Want to see photos?*

I never understood why salmon was special to mom until she explained.

"Your generation would never understand but it was a luxury!" Mom rolled her eyes in ecstasy. "Salmon used to be expensive. When this 3D meat came out, people were all sorts of funky. Some people thought you'd get fat or get cancer. But all of a sudden, the homeless man on the corner was eating better food than Napoleon. It was like Jesus takin' air and breaking it into twelve fish."

"Breakfast CLP with cheddar cheese and white bread bagel," the automated cashier brought me back to the present. "Would you like a creamy cappuccino with that?"

That's not within your budget, Cort reminded me. It smelt of luxurious roasted coffee topped with clouds of cream.

"Oh, I can't resist." I said to the cash register, indirectly justifying the purchase to Cort. Good thing robo-assistants can't pass judgment.

"Would you like a side of fruit with the rest of your meal?"

The screen showed me a display of round purple grapes, dewy from condensation. I could almost feel the juice of the grapes in my mouth.

"No, thank you." I said, swallowing hard.

"Your total was charged to your account. Thank you and visit us at Che's again."

I stepped aside to wait for my order and scrolled on my Cort tablet through my social feed, my matching feed, and my news feed, when a shimmer of red suddenly caught my eye. A woman in her fifties ordered and then stood aside. She crossed her arms with a scrunched face.

"Order seventy-five, your food is located in the serving window." I flinched at the sound of my order number and rose to stand. The woman in red strutted to the window with determination and grabbed the bag along with a cup of coffee.

I was taken aback. *Maybe she doesn't know it's my order?*

The woman in red turned around with the food bag, looking through me as if I were glass.

You're not grabbing that? questioned Cort, but as I opened my mouth, her heels were clicking toward the exit.

Was I wrong about my order number?

Hungry and regretting my hesitancy, I waited for a human cashier to assist with my missing order. I was flustered, and perhaps that singular event catalyzed how much of a disaster the rest of the day would be.

I adopted a sense of urgency as I felt time slipping away. I paced myself through elevators and escalators until I found a self-help desk.

"Good morning," I tried catching my breath. "I'm looking for Paul Mcguire?"

Three dots appeared on the screen, thinking over my words. "Okay. You'll need to head back into the break room. Head straight and make a right at the welcome sign."

The break room itself was full of different types of discolored maps, disassembled navigational devices, scrambled flight equipment, and suits covered with grime. I couldn't see anyone being able to have a "break" in this room; the floor had dark stains on it, the air felt sticky, and crumbs were scattered on the floor.

Over one screen stood a sharp-jawed man, his bushy eyebrows scrunched up. He looked young and old at the same time, maybe in his late thirties. He was well dressed, and his cunning eyes hid behind stylish eyeglasses. His shiny, bald head glimmered under the beaming office lights as if he were the star of the show. When I stepped into the room, he looked up at me in acknowledgment, examining me without a change in facial expression.

"Good morning. You must be Aryana." He reached out a thin bony hand for me to shake, which displayed a thick golden band on his finger. "I'm Paul. Pleased to meet you. Give me one minute."

"Nice to meet you too" I said. *Now, how do I make the best first impression?* I wondered, but Paul looked down and away from me. He clicked some buttons on his screen, paused, and typed some more.

This guy lacks tact. Cort said the exact comment I had thought.

I felt the urge to pull together the silence by checking my Cort tablet but decided that would make a poor first impression.

Once Paul was done with his task, he looked up and smiled at me with sharpened, pearly teeth.

"I was told by your human recruiter that you moved for this job," he said with distant admiration. "That's quite the dedication and that's what we look for at NK Air."

Don't let him throw you off. Cort advised. *Be confident.*

"I've wanted to work here for a long time." I said, sinking into my own thoughts. This job was my attempt at being an adult, or at least acting like one. "It seems good for—"

"Glad to have you on the team," he cut me off. "Anyway, let me tell you about how we run here. I am your director of operations. I make the final calls, make schedules, and make sure that everyone is doing what they are supposed to. You are going to be trained by nurse Lorraine. She's a sweet lady—easy to work with. Oh, and while we are on the topic, we strictly prohibit any internal gimmicks or robo-assistants, not that you could afford one though?"

Heat rose through my cheeks. Cort hummed in my ear. I shook my head from how flustered and caught off guard I was.

"Now, I like operations to work efficiently. Wasting time wastes the company's money. It derails us from our mission, which is to provide quality care with zero mistakes." Paul sat back in a chair, interlocking his thick hands over his stomach. "You can lock up your belongings, meet the staff, and then come out to the meeting. I do expect you to be early this time." He locked eyes with me as my chest tightened. I nodded my head, blinking to break away the relentless eye contact.

"I'm not familiar with this hospital," I mumbled. Paul picked up a cup of energizing fluids to make a loud sucking sound.

"It shouldn't be that hard to find if you had used the self-guided location app. If you step out into the hallway and make a left to the door beside the linen closet, you should be able to locate it."

A loud warning sign flashed on almost all the navigational screens, accompanied by a wailing siren. Paul switched his attention to the buttons on a panel, put in a couple of passwords, and the warning signs were pacified. He laughed with his mouth but not with his eyes. I tried my best to make my face look as calm as possible, but the unexpected thrill of the siren had made me uneasy.

"What was I saying?" Paul cocked his head to the side. "I'll see you in twenty."

I stumbled out of the helpless break room to find the lockers.

What a weird guy, Cort thought to me as I packed away my bags and applied fingerprints to lock the door.

I don't think I've ever made such a poor first impression, I thought. *It's an hour before shift starts. I came as promised.*

Take some deep breaths, Cort advised. *You're getting ahead of yourself. By the way, you made your locker's password "one, two, three, four," in case you forgot.*

I've wanted to work here, but Lord knows I want to quit right this second. At that moment, I realized blood from my finger had left a brown trail all over the locker's touch screen. I had picked the skin around my nails raw without even noticing.

CHAPTER 3

THE HALF-LIMPING HELICOPTER

———

I opened the door to overwhelmingly bright light, a roar of machines, and the rancid smell of oil. The helipad was a huge, football-sized field with three grownup versions of children's toy aircrafts standing ready to run.

According to the site How to Make Great First Impressions, they mentioned to always introduce yourself first and offer a helping hand. There's probably some preliminary work for you to do, Cort pleasantly reminded me.

Shut up. I told her.

Will do.

An elderly gentleman was cursing over a circular piece of metal with wires and wrenches scattered around. He noticed that I had reached the helipad platform and we accidentally made eye contact. I nodded over the din of the helicopter. He stood up groaning over his knees and approached me with importance lying on his broad shoulders.

"The name's Lucas," he yelled, keeping his dirty hands to the side. "I'm a pilot here." I tried introducing myself in return, but he waved his arm. "You're the rookie on my crew,

I know." He nodded, clicking some button that turned off the din. "Hope that we will work well together."

"It's an honor to be here." I said, forgetting about the dirt and shaking his grimy hand. I know people love to talk about themselves after working with the public for years, so I added. "Have you worked here for a while?"

"I've been a pilot for thirty years in different facets." Lucas picked through his white mustache. I felt sorry for anyone who would have to kiss him. "I used to be more on the engineering side. You heard of Sol Flight?"

Lucas was not an exception to that psychological trick. I could tell that it didn't matter whether I knew what Sol Flight was, but what did matter was that I would listen to anything he said.

"Maybe." I said, but that's all the ignition needed.

"Well, I was designing their solar run batteries for aircraft. I was even working on air vehicles for the consumer population, but that was a stretch." Lucas wrinkled his nose.

"Interesting." I lied. "Why was it a stretch?"

"Eh. I like work and processes to go my way, you know?" he admitted. "I have a tried-and-true system. I've been an engineer for as long as I can remember. I can put together a phone in two hours." Lucas held up two thick fingers. Both of us were startled as his pager bleeped.

Lucas cursed, pointing to the beeping device attached at the hip of his flight suit. "You know what that is? Some bad news. This pump is hardly functioning and I still gotta fly it. Welcome to NK Air."

"Wow," I murmured, not sure whether to take his comment as a lighthearted joke or some serious commentary. I didn't have a chance to ask though, as a moment later I noticed a short, full woman—with colorful badges across her breast pocket—approaching us. By the time the pilot noticed her too, she was only feet away from us. As if it were a secret language, she rolled her eyes at him in greeting. She looked noticeably tired to the point where her bronze makeup couldn't conceal the violet eye bags.

"Great, the rookie's here." The woman outstretched her hand to me with a corner of a tattoo sleeve peeking out. "Lorraine. I'm your preceptor. This is our 'copter, the S-440. It doesn't work 30 percent of the time, but that doesn't mean that we have the option to not take this call."

"The helicopter doesn't work?" I stuttered, but a helmet had been shoved into my arms.

"Rookie, fill the pump with fluid," Lucas shoved a heavy canister into my chest, pointed at a nozzle door, and powered on the helicopter again. I spilled the clear fluid all over the cemented helipad.

"That was pathetic. Anyway, the call should be near the bog," Lorraine shouted at Lucas. I prayed the canister wouldn't slip out of my fingers as it sloshed into the pump.

"Rookie, get in!"

Lorraine had already disappeared inside the S-440, so I followed to squeeze myself in the tight aircraft entrance. An angry-toned alarm pulsed the S-440 like a battalion march. Sitting down to buckle myself, I exhaled a huge breath to counteract the horridly stressed fight-or-flight mode I was in. *This is it*, I thought with excitement. *This is the start of a new era—a new Ary.*

Lorraine vehemently signaled at her head. I reached up to the keypad on my headset and fingered for a button. I could feel the helicopter revving upwards but then struggling to go up with more force.

"Try again." Lorraine yelled into the headset. I wasn't quite sure if that was for me, but I found a circular button to press on. I recognized Paul's clean-cut accent over the headset.

"S-440, you are responding to a forty-year-old female. She has cancer and is in need of treatment. Time is 6:49."

"S-440 preparing for liftoff." Lucas replied into the headset.

"S-440 lifting off. Have a good morning. 6:50."

The helicopter lifted off, this time with more confidence.

"Good. You figured it out," Lorraine's voice echoed into my headset. "Take a look at what's in here for a second to familiarize yourself."

The body of the helicopter was a compact space with equipment worth two mansions. Near the stretcher was a long bench that had equipment piled on top of itself. I recognized the standard equipment of portable ventilators, a cardiac monitor, and oxygen tanks, but there was also a blood sample analyzer, a portable ultrasound mini tech, and a robot for CPR.

"You wanna look out the window?" Lorraine asked, but I shook my head. My stomach was spinning in circles. She laughed.

"To continue our on-the-spot training," Lorraine said, "We are a tad superstitious here. There's a forbidden word that starts with a 'c' and rhymes with 'rash.' In the case of that—" Lorraine pointed at a red button next to me. "Click it."

The helicopter swayed from side to side. Lucas audibly cursed.

Adrenaline is a hormone that takes a lot to achieve, but it's like a gory, gushing artery bleed once it's activated. It flows heavily and is challenging to control, especially for someone neurotic like me.

~

The patient was a pale and frail woman by the name of Hanna, worn down by the poison in her body. She was bald, on supplemental oxygen, and introduced herself through thin lips to warn us that too much movement caused a lot of pain in her. And no wonder: she had recurrent episodes of cancer. Cancer in the breast twenty years ago, then a lymphoma ten years ago. This decade, it was pancreatic cancer. She was being transported to a higher-level facility for genetic treatment that would have a slim chance of helping prevent her from getting more cancer.

Although Lorraine carried a professional demeanor, there was still a numb ice wall between her and the patient. She went through the robotic motions of introducing herself and then me as the student. To Hanna, this didn't matter much; she had already seen plenty of people in scrubs care less.

Lorraine tasked me with starting a second IV in her, which was simple enough with such a bony patient with bruises left over from previous pokes on her dry, wrinkled arms. Still, it had been a while since I had used my skill. I palpated her knuckles, feeling a sweat break out on my forehead. I tried to visualize the channels and bones and muscles. The bounce of the vein! I double checked and with glee angled the tiny catheter until the flash went through.

After successfully completing the assigned task, I looked at Lorraine for confirmation. She only shrugged her shoulders.

"Let's move."

Packaging Hanna for transport was another difficult beast. It caused a decent amount of stress in Hanna to be jostled and rolled like a package of bones and skin, even if she didn't yell out in pain. She wasn't heavy either, but the number of wires and monitors and IV lines easily tangled into a clump. In my eyes, Hanna was a delicate flower being supported only by the care of her metallic roots and branches.

Lucas had stayed behind by the S-440 and looked considerably distressed. After securing the patient inside the S-440, Lorraine motioned to me to jump into the S-440 while she stepped aside. I sat in silence with Hanna as she had her eyes closed and her hands resting over her chest like she was ready for a coffin. The heart monitor beeped in an irregular pattern, the oxygen tubing hissed, and I could hear Lorraine heatedly talking outside.

Don't sit in silence, talk to her! Cort scolded me.

"How have you been entertaining yourself?" I asked Hanna to draw attention away from chaos. Hanna's eyes fluttered open for a brief second.

"I sleep a lot." She said hoarsely. "Sometimes listen to music."

Hannah closed her eyes again. I could hear Lucas now outside.

"When I did my daily check of the S-440 today, I didn't know that flying a half-ass helicopter was part of the list!" Lorraine was clearly upset.

Tense and unsure, I decided to focus on my strength of small talk. "What type of music do you like to listen to?"

"Hymns are good." Hanna dry-coughed and kept her eyes closed. I took this as a sign to let the poor woman suffer in peace. Lorraine stepped into the helicopter, fuming.

This time, the S-440 did lift off. We had a smooth and quiet flight to our destination. After delivering Hanna to the hospital, I excused myself to the bathroom to have a quiet moment, fix my hair, and continue to the next patient.

CHAPTER 4

FUELING MORTALITY

Lunch break didn't feel like lunch break. It felt like I was back in school to write an elaborate report on what happened with Hanna the patient. Lorraine sat behind me with her hands crossed while chomping on a medium-grade sandwich. Lorraine told me to manually write the report even though Cort or any program could have easily written the report within two minutes. Cort took a backseat and played a peaceful playlist meant to "stimulate the brain."

"Keep writing, Alyana." Lucas mispronounced my name. I bit back my tongue with resentment.

Lucas had taken a break from fixing the S-440, propping up his mud-covered boots onto the table. *Disgusting*, I thought to myself while looking out of the corner of my eye.

"Working at this company, you have a menu of bullshit," Lucas laughed darkly. "Either you get your poison choice of cancer, or you get your hardly flying S-440."

Lorraine was dumbfoundedly clicking a pen with a thousand-mile stare.

"Unbelievable. We have had ten minutes of a break," Lucas turned on the news as we sat in silence. On the screens in the break room, dramatic, ominous music played while thick clouds rolled around the screen. The news blared of the oncoming tropical storm with "freezing rain, high wind speeds, and flash flooding." "I hope we aren't flying when that thing rolls in," Lucas muttered under his breath, then turned with conviction to Lorraine, as if suddenly remembering something. "Lo, what has gotten into you today? You were supposed to finish the special reports from last week."

Lorraine shook her head and waved a careless hand. "I'll get to them soon enough."

"You're ain't the type to forget." Lucas noted as Lorraine sat staring with disinterest at her lunch.

Did I miss something? I asked.

Shh. Cort hissed into my ear. *Let it unravel on its own.* Lorraine sighed and turned to me with a look of pity.

"Today is a bad, bad anniversary." she said with hesitation pulling away at her tongue.

"Is it that day?" Lucas looked away from his entertainment. Lorraine smoothed back a loose curl with a pin.

"Yes," she said softly. "I woke up and remembered that my baby girl would've been ten years old, as of today. I lit an old-fashioned candle for her this morning."

"I'm so sorry." I stammered, unsure of what to say, watching Lorraine picking through her poufy hair. *Just as I expected.* Cort whispered. The principle of "if you don't ask, you'll never know" was huge with Cort usage.

"I was having a girl, but then one day, I woke up and I couldn't shake the feeling that she was dead. My hubby took me to the hospital. The doctors did an ultrasound, and I could immediately tell there was no movement. It was so obvious."

Lorraine picked out the 3D black-and-white image of her. "She'd be so big by now." Lorraine bit her lip with a look of worry, showing us the picture.

Thankfully, Lucas jumped in this time to mediate the uncomfortable silence.

"Let's get you a beer after work," he said.

"I already planned on that, Lucas. Coming to this job is enough reason for me to drink." Lorraine laughed with tears in her eyes.

They laughed at her dark joke. I must've looked horrified because Lorraine tried to reassure me.

"Don't worry, my Cort provides me with a personalized therapy program," she said. "It's been a long journey to convince myself that none of what happened was my fault and to move past that. Now I have two sons, a daughter, and a tiny angel that I miss."

A wave of grief washed over me, causing my chest to tighten. It was asking to be cast away and to explode into an enormous flowing waterfall.

"What's wrong?" a blurred voice in the background asked out of politeness. I was like a shaking tower that was close to collapsing. At first, I stammered, unable to find the right words.

"I've also recently gone through a death," I mustered out of myself. "My mom died a month ago."

"I'm so sorry." Lorraine said with sympathy. "That happened with some terrible timing for you."

We sat there together in sentimental silence; Lorraine was picking through old ultrasound photos and I was lost in thoughts.

She sighed.

"Well now, it looks like it might be a busy day," said Lorraine, dabbing at her eyes. "Go on and finish that report. Something tells me that it may be a busy day today."

And she was right. The pager beeped its ominous tone and I rushed to finish my thoughts. Unlike the last time a call was released, Lorraine didn't leave me to fluster and stumble in the dark. She explained that the standard approach to every dispatched call was to receive a sparse amount of information as a way of preventing emotion from clouding bias.

"Say there's a patient with the same rare disease that your best friend had. A crew would be more inclined to take the call regardless of the associated risks," Lorraine explained.

"The S-440 isn't fixed but the timer has already started." Lucas scratched his beard. "It's far away from the city's boundaries."

People rarely visit north of NK City—considered an uninhabited land with savages. They were known to be morally corrupt, raised animals for killing, and had to be kept at hand by a surveillance force (the surveillance force is a body of robots intended for the security and protection of NK City's citizens). Every self-preservation instinct in my body was rebelling against this idea, yet this was my first day, and my companions seemed to be confident—or so it seemed at first, as Lorraine's face was now wrinkled with concern.

"Is there no option to refuse taking a call?" I asked. Lucas laughed crudely.

"Come on rookie, at this company, we take any wild card we can get."

"Lucas, what was the risk assessment for this trip?" Lorraine asked.

We peered into his screen as the program ran a calculation. A bold 52 percent was shown, glowing an encouraging green light at us. Lucas grimaced and took a deep inhale of his vaporizer.

"The risk assessment is high, but it's still telling us to take the trip?" I thought out loud.

"It must be well paying," said Lorraine.

"I want to go home and play Minerva with my grandkids. This sounds like a bad idea." Lucas echoed my thoughts as a call request from Paul popped up on the screen. Lucas answered the call. (Minerva is a virtual reality game featuring the mythology of an almighty goddess controlling Greek heroes' bodies while fighting multiple battles from Troy, Antioch, and Anatolia.)

Paul's odious, shiny head reflected through the screen.

"That's a poor attitude to have, Lucas." Paul put on a tense smile. My hairs stood up in goosebumps from Paul listening in to our conversation. *Isn't that weird? What else does this guy do to his coworkers?* Lucas huffed into Paul's reflection.

"There's no reason to hide from you that the risk assessment is dismal," Lorraine explained in a matter-of-fact way. It made me feel giddy to see a confrontation between the short, stocky Lorraine and the lanky Paul.

"Doll, calm down." Paul said, his hands raised in the air like it was a trick taught in business school. "This is your job. I looked at my route calculation programs, and it doesn't seem that it would be a bad trip."

Lucas clenched his teeth into a groan.

"Paul, with all due respect, I don't care what your little program said," Lucas snapped back. "I've got grandkids and a great wife to think of. I am a professional pilot. If something doesn't seem right, I don't want it."

Paul used a skinny, long nail to push his black-framed glasses up his nose, gearing up for a harsh comeback. He resorted to keeping his composure though, knowing that yelling back was the fight Lucas wanted.

"You say you're a professional. I pull eighty-hour work weeks while you come in for three days and hardly work twelve hours? Come on now."

"That's not true. I've been working five days over since you can't even keep more than three pilots employed!" Lucas's spit gleamed iridescently on the screen.

"Paul, we'll be glad to work on any other trip," Lorraine mixed in a voice of reason. "Besides, today we are focusing on training with Aryana."

Needless to say, I was pleased that Lorraine knew my real name even if I went by a shorter nickname.

Paul smoothed a singular, stranded hair that had fallen out of place from the piles of gloopy hair gel. This irritated Lucas even more.

"You seem to think that a job is worth killing yourself over and put this same expectation on the rest of us." Lucas yelled at the flat screen, reminiscent of an angry viking cartoon. "Do I need to remind you that, fundamentally, we do different jobs?"

Paul cleared his throat and took out nicotine gum to munch on. The paper crackled. I heard the familiar beeping of a smart watch, warning him to calm down despite his face's eerie rigidity.

"You need to quit making excuses that are based on meager chances." Paul's thin lips narrowed into a tube. "Instead of being a burden on us, be a team player—earn your paycheck."

The contrasting storms had created a thunderclap headache for me. Lucas was unrelenting, monologuing about how he wished he could retire but couldn't, how Paul could take his own private jet and fly himself out of this world, how Paul was a "crackhead bastard only in it for the coin," and how ancient Lucas was—all intertwined with curse words.

Although I had agreed with Lucas, Lorraine seemed annoyed with Lucas's self-pitying, and Paul's cool swayed me.

"Let's make a decision. The sooner we move out of here, the more likely we are to beat that storm," Lorraine interrupted Lucas on his strings of cursing.

Lucas grumbled something softly about a paycheck, then turned to me with a grimace. "What does the rookie think?" He glared at me.

I felt no authority to speak. I was already exhausted and overwhelmed with new information. I shrugged my shoulders. Paul stared at me with an unrelenting gaze through the distance of the screen.

What would mother say? She would take the risk in a heartbeat. But is this a grave mistake?

It's fifty-fifty, Cort mentioned.

"Anything goes," I said, recognizing how stupid I sounded. "And weather calculations aren't always accurate. Storms move around."

"Good," said Paul. "I'll let them know you are coming."

Paul ultimately had the last, fatal word.

~

The noise of the rotor blades grew louder and louder as Lucas and Lorraine yelled orders into the headset. I was scrambling to follow along, but each command in the unfamiliar aircraft left me more frazzled.

"Load the liquid oxygen."

"You're slowing us down, rookie." I felt my chest tighten and hot blood rise into my cheeks as I huffed my strength away to shove the metal canister into the compartment.

"Get the fuel!" Lucas yelled at me.

"Where is that?" Lucas waved me into the direction of the concrete building.

I knew I had seen little tugging robots with red fuel canisters. After seeing such a robotic creature on its way away from the helipad, I broke into a run, pulling the dirty canister out of its possession. I handed the canister back to Lucas.

"How's the storm looking?" I asked Lucas, handing the fuel to him. He ignored me out of spite.

"If the rookie keeps movin' like a slug, we gon' hit the storm," Lucas addressed Lorraine with his sardonic comment.

"I finished the rest of the checklist. Buckle in," Lorraine yelled. I followed her inside the body, seated across from her as she strapped herself in and adjusted her helmet. The straps rested snuggly over my shoulders and chest.

"NK Tower, S-440 preparing liftoff, northwest bound," Lucas grumbled into the microphone.

"S-440 cleared for liftoff. Twelve-o-five. Good day."

The higher up the S-440 went, the smaller my familiar world became. Domestic shuttles looked like metal snakes from up above. Air vehicles seemed to become slower and slower. The skyscrapers of NK City became tiny gray blocks in the background, the neon commercial lights outlining the structures.

The initial minutes of liftoff were peaceful under the lull of the rotor blades. That was until we hit the promised icy rain.

There are some moments that happen too quickly to register, the S-440 crash being one of them. Mom's impending death lasted two years and I expected it. But these ten minutes became flash memories I would never forget.

The S-440 swung from side to side like an angry dragon's tail. A strange drumming rhythm could be heard from the ice pellets attacking the S-440. Through the tiny window, I could see the S-440's shadow crawling in the trees below. We were falling too fast. I averted my eyes from the window and clung tightly to the seatbelt. Lucas cursed loudly into the headset, then started giving a long-winded air report over the roar of S-440's rotor blades.

Lorraine had long closed her eyes, both of her hands on her chest. I couldn't tell if she was gasping for air or praying with a dramatic flair.

"I'm going to try and land. Might be rough," Lucas's voice crackled in the headset.

I grasped onto a handle, trying to steady myself against the terrifying speed at which we were flying into treetops. Now this is one bad dream.

The S-440 hit the ground with a bang. It flipped over and over again, each impact throwing my spine back. Finally, the heaviness of the S-440 stopped the velocity of the crash.

I heard the most horrible sound of crumpling metal and then eerie stillness.

CHAPTER 5

BONES AND ROCK

———

An icy drizzle rapped upon the metal, waking me up. A buzzing rang through my ears. But when I came to, I realized I was in my worst nightmare.

I was strapped in my seat, stuck upside down. The pens, IVs, and coins I kept pocketed had slipped out and fallen onto the S-440's ceiling. They cunningly shined at me like distant stars.

What would have been Lorraine's previous seat was directly across from me. But Lorraine was battered in the metallic arms of the S-440. The ceiling of the S-440 had sunken into her helmet, pushing her neck down. A stream of blood had dried onto her neck.

"Hey," I rasped toward Lorraine, but she didn't budge. The seatbelt and helmet were collectively choking me out. But if I were to unfasten my seat belt, gravity would push me directly onto Lorraine and hurt her even more.

I couldn't even tell if she was alive.

I tried calling out her name but instead coughed loudly.

"Lorraine, come on," I rasped, clearing my throat and coughing again. Maybe the headset still worked. "Lucas, hello?"

There was no response from the other end. The world was spinning from lack of oxygen and my heart rhythm was beating an anxious, tachycardic beat.

"I'm going to unstrap and fall on you," I rasped to Lorraine. I unclipped the seatbelt and fell on top of her in a heap, right onto my elbow. My arm radiated electric pain, causing me to howl. This was probably the instant I caused the sprain in my elbow, which only became worse with time.

Dammit, dammit, dammit! The arm's pain burned like crazy.

But Lorraine had shifted, shaking her head from one side to the other. Minding my arm, I lifted the helmet off her. Lorraine's nose was slowly leaking blood out. Her eyes flickered open, unfocused and dilated.

"Gimme a bag," she whispered, a small tear rolling down her face. I unbuckled her to give her more space to move in. After handing her a red biohazard bag, she heaved the contents out of her stomach.

"What hurts?" I asked her.

"My head, dammit." I palpated around her head as she vomited some more. A mild bruise above her left eye was forming.

"How bad?" I asked. "Enough for pain meds?"

Lorraine groaned and leaned back, nodding slowly.

"Anything else I can do for you?" I asked, tapping into my nurse personality. Lorraine waved her hand away as a universal "don't bother me" sign. "I'll check on Lucas then."

I kicked out the back door from the S-440, but I easily lost my balance and ended up slipping and falling onto the grass. My neck hurt mildly, but the worst pain was in my throbbing arm. I would have loved to fall asleep forever on the grass while rain buried me away, but the pain constantly jabbed at me. *Get up, stupid.* The pain mocked me.

The S-440's tail was smoking dully in the rain with blades bent into odd angles. The side that Lorraine had been seated in became contorted and smashed. Seeing a view that should have killed Lorraine and myself was horrifying. I wondered how the crash had impacted Lucas.

I tried to use my arms to pull my body up but felt an immediate hot electric shock again in the elbow. I fell onto my back and tried to scream, but I couldn't catch my breath.

Cort's connection was static and nonexistent, but even then, I knew she would have said something along the lines of:

Take three deep breaths. Would you like a calming mantra to repeat?

The first breath was shallow, and I coughed. The second felt easier, and the third one I released with ease.

I can't use my left arm. I'm having trouble breathing, but that could also be the adrenaline. I can try rolling onto my right arm to pull myself up.

Knees shaking, I stood up. I rolled around my heel, testing what posture was less painful. I limped once, then limped another step closer to the cockpit.

I could see Lucas's figure in the cockpit, his helmet pressed into the headrest. The door had busted away from the frame.

"Lucas," I coughed into the smoking air. His red-veined eyes flickered, and he groaned. I shook him with my painful arm. Nothing seemed wrong with him except that his hands were covered in pink, burnt flesh. Nasty pus was pooling around. He moved his lips and coughed.

"What?" I moved my ear closer to him and raised the visor of his helmet off. "Save your breath. Help me move you out of here."

With my strong working arm, I put his arms around my neck and tugged in the direction out of the smoking cockpit. I was happy to see that his strength was still intact, and he was able to stand on his legs with no deadweight on me. He hobbled around and out of the S-440.

"Help me get your helmet off, will you?" I asked him, unstrapping it.

"Damn, this itchy." He groaned, itching at the patches of dirt that had dug into the wrinkles on his face. I cringed at the sight of his hands.

"Looks like your hands are burned. Once I wrap them up, I need your help getting Lorraine out," I told him. "Do you have anything to extricate her out of the metal frame?"

Lucas raised an eyebrow at me. "She look alive?"

"She's awake but groggy," I said. Lucas fingered the outline of his burns despite my warning. "I wouldn't touch that," I said with hesitancy, thinking of how unpleasant an infection in the wild would be. Lucas snapped his neck up at me.

"Lo better be a dead woman," he said. "I can't believe that woman is such a pushover for a freakin' raise! That man could tell her to jump off a parachute and that's exactly—"

Over Lucas's angry rant, I observed how disturbing the S-440 looked. It was shocking we survived that crash. The helicopter's nose had folded into itself, and the paint was charred. The tail end was twisted, the rotor blades were scattered, the body was battered, and Lorraine's side had a huge concave indent from the oak tree nearby. The air vehicle was surrounded by the shade of the canopies. The S-440 was a scrimpy defense from the wind; leaks of dew leached in through the cracks, which we later learned would cause our sheets to be perpetually damp. The cracked glass of the windows circulated wild fresh air, which cooled the S-440 at night.

Lucas cringed at the sight of my swollen elbow. The adrenaline was wearing down to be replaced by a thumping headache. With my deformed arm in a poorly constructed sling and Lucas's burns hardly wrapped taut, we put up a struggle to pull Lorraine out. She lay in a daze in the stretcher, alert but looking exhausted. "I'm okay, I'm okay," she told us every few minutes.

Lucas sat outside in the rain with relief for a smoke. Surrounding the S-440 was a glossy covering of shrubbery and trees, their collective shadows casting cold weather over us. It smelt of the S-440's putrid gas and the cleansed earth. Frogs cried from their mudding houses. I sat down across from this view beside Lucas.

"Do you think we have a good chance of getting back?" I asked him, fiddling with Cort's earpieces.

"In the S-440? No way, the nose blasted itself when we hit ground." Lucas coughed on his smoke. *Did he not breathe in enough of that garbage air in the cockpit?* "The engine and fuel on Lorraine's side were also impacted. That crosses flying out."

Here I thought you were some top-notch engineer, I thought to myself.

"The program screens melted and gave me these lovely burns." He wiggled his bandaged fingers. "No point of contact with base."

"What about through Cort?" I asked, restarting the pearly earbuds. She made a wailing noise on loudspeaker.

"I'm sorry. I can't access the network. Please try again later," Cort said to me. I was shocked at her reaction because I had never seen such an error happen with her. Cort was the all-knowing best friend and had never denied me anything. I felt betrayed by my best friend.

"What an amateur," Lucas mocked, picking at the gauze wrappings around his burns. "There's no connection out here."

"Cort, what do I do?" I asked. "Where are we?"

Cort hesitated.

"I'm sorry, I didn't quite catch that. I can upload your questions to a cloud and answer when I'm back online, if you'd like."

"Just give it up." Lucas shivered. "There's no connection out here whatsoever."

I switched off the earbuds, watching the battery light dim.

"What's the plan now?"

I jumped from the unexpected, soft voice. It was Lorraine's figure, wrapped in an emergency foil blanket and presenting herself as a walking triangle. "Can we crack open the drug box? My headache is killing me."

"There's never been an emergency plan." Lucas grumbled. "There was no 'what if' when you signed up for this job. Our management couldn't care less about resolving such problems. In their eyes, we're just fired folk who'll get replaced by some bright-eyed deer while we're smoked out here by the outside folk or the surveillance force."

"What are the chances that a surveillance force will rescue us?" I asked. Lucas shrugged.

"For one, it's a mystery what they look like. Some say they look like that extinct species. Although, I can't remember the names—I'm terrible with names." Lucas paused. "Bald eagle, was it? And two, I've heard that the surveillance forces are brutal, not tolerant of people who venture out."

"If the surveillance forces aren't friendly, and my Cort is down, then what are our options for other means of communication?" I asked.

Lucas stroked his beard as he ran through the list: there were the satellite communications, tactical radios, and VPNs. He gave us a tour of the melted dark screens, what used to be perfect rectangular covers turned into twisted frames and discolored wires. Lucas was confident in his abilities to make contact with society if he had a chance to fix.

I tried to pay attention to the magical feats Lucas would have to jump through to fix the satellite communications while hunger, thirst, arm pain, and fatigue all weighed on my mind.

"Oh, dear," Lorraine leaned against the frayed metal, clutching at her chest with her free hand. "As long as we stay around the S-440's ruins, we can hold out hope that a rescue force will come back for us."

~

We decided that the standard rules applying to drugs didn't count during a plane crash. After each of us received an equal, low-dose portion of pain medicine intravenously, we had a dinner of our cold-packed rations. It was clear that Lucas was hiding food packed by his wife because he kept hiding something. Lorraine knew him too well and convinced him to share food if she shared her packed beer. Despite eating cold leftover salmon, sitting wrapped in a shared foil blanket and sharing a meal with others while feeling euphoria from morphine was comforting. Nothing mattered, there was no more pain, no lack of Cort. Everything was perfect.

Sipping at their beer bottles, Lorraine and Lucas were less relaxed than I was.

"I can't wait for the rescue to come. Boy, are we going to make a rag out of Paul Mcguire." Lorraine giggled and leaned back unsteadily, either because of being drunk or high. "I'm going to blow away all the money."

"I hope you don't pour it all into your real estate business, you stupid wench," Lucas insulted. Although Lorraine was used to Lucas's disrespect, she raised a matter-of-a-fact finger.

"I'll have you know that my real estate business is still successful," Lorraine retorted.

"Why do you run a business when you're successful at your job?" I asked.

"That was not the point of me moving into real estate." Lorraine frowned. "I've been a nurse for twenty years and I feel it. I feel it in my back, in my swollen feet, and my cursed bladder. Management wants this, management wants that, and on top of what they want, I have my patients' wants. My needs to eat normally and have a break? No, they don't care."

"Typical burnout," I said.

"Obviously. But I'm in so deep." Lorraine took a swig of her beer dramatically. "This whole catastrophe is the final straw. Once we win the case, I'm putting all of the money into my business. Maybe some drugs on the side—this morphine is a little too good," she joked.

"This all happened because of Paul," Lucas drunkenly exclaimed, clearly not listening to Lorraine's woes, but at least he forgave her by then. "We have to get that man back!"

"You watch me. We're going to milk him for money." Lorraine laughed.

"We should make a blood pact," Lucas said, reaching for my finger. I laughed without a care, letting him pull my finger. It seemed the anger against Paul was unifying us and dissolving our hierarchy. "I could find something safe to prick ourselves with, we can start the pact tonight!"

Lorraine cleared her throat dramatically. "We need to talk about our story—have the worst possible version that we all agree on."

"Lighten up Lo." Lucas handed her beer bottle back. "Once we get back, it'll be easy to frame Paul. Imagine the compensation! I'll retire."

Soon enough, the morphine high died down, and the gravity of being stuck in the woods without any working lamps set in.

The sunlight was gone, and we were sleepy anyway, ready to pick out our corner of the S-440 to sleep in.

The drizzle of stars on the night sky is a romantic idea, but the vastness of the dark and lack of manmade lights was terrifying and isolating—a reminder that we were alone without the lights of communicating airplanes. I yearned for the bustle of Broad Highway with the crowds of people mixed with their robotic assistants, the vendors handing out buttered crisp street food, the stinging bright lights of stores beckoning a second look. I could steal glances at the fashionable business owners with their freshly shined loafers while watching the tails of their ulsters flying behind their ambitions.

From every point of the city, I could see the rings of the gubernatorial buildings outlined by strings of lights.

One time my mother and I visited a modern art museum with a planetarium exhibit. I could see the golden planets, stars, the ISS. And after feeling like a tiny E. coli cell in the observatory exhibit, I could exit out and step back into comfort after blinking to the bright lights. I missed that feeling of security that the woods did not present. Besides, the woods had no controllable thermostat; bugs pricked and buzzed, and there was no nice way to wipe myself other than leaves. And the silence amplified any small creak or branch rustle. Time was slower than a dead man rolling in his grave.

CHAPTER 6

DREAMING OF WATER

"Ary." My mother gasped, the nasal cannula sagging out of her nose. I fixed the tubing back into her nostril.

"What ma?"

She opened her thin lips into a suggestion, then set them back into a wrinkle under her darkened lip hair. I knew what she was about to say—it was a terrible itch on the tip of her tongue.

"I'm sick of being in pain." she groaned. "I'm an eternally lying statue—can't move on my own. So useless. I'm a burden." She coughed out her smoker lungs, then exhaled with a wheeze. "I wish you'd help me die."

My heart flipped and I shook my head with subtlety. I could see my mother's eyes dilate and the contour turn into a ghastly look. I didn't expect her to be able to move, but her hands had latched onto my throat in a move to choke me. I struggled for air.

"Let me drink!" I yelled at her. "Let me drink!"

Lorraine tapped me out of my dream. "Quit sleep talkin'!"

I curled into a tighter fetal position, throwing off the emergency foil blanket. While the night had been extremely cold, the S-440 became a tin greenhouse that amplified the heat. My mouth was the driest of sponges, emitting the nasty odor of acetone. I regretted the heavy hammer headache from last night's beer. I only wanted the carnal pleasure of pouring spring water into my mouth.

The three of us had claimed a different piece of the S-440. Lucas, in hopes of hearing any traffic from the radios, had stationed himself in the cockpit like an all-hearing watchdog. Referring to her chronic back pain, Lorraine took the cushioned stretcher while I outstretched on the hard bench. Privilege of the youth, as she said.

We were still confident that we would be found. Lucas had scared me with stories of vigilante surveillance forces in the woods, but both Lorraine and I were hoping for a rescue team to find us. None of the radios worked, which tasked Lucas to tinker with the radio in his meaty hands.

Hardly any sunshine grazed our campsite, and while it hadn't rained since the crash, the air was moist with the smell of juicy roots, dewy water vapor, and the vanishing morning fog. Nevertheless, I was pleased with the scarce sun rays that peaked through the pillar of trees—some light was better than pitch-black darkness.

Finding my water bottle empty and my packed food having evaporated into crumbs was an unpleasant surprise. My inventory included lotion, an empty plastic bag for lunch, a dead Cort, Cort's extra hardware, a charger for Cort, a portable screen, an empty water bottle, a hairbrush, lip balm, an old-fashioned notebook, a pen running out of ink, hand sanitizer, and trauma shears. Lorraine presented her own pack: an empty coffee mug, lipstick, retouching powder, lotion, pictures of her kids, all the gear for her Cort, and hair oil.

Needless to say, our collective inventory was ill suited for longer survival. I didn't need Cort to tell me that dehydration would kill me faster than hunger.

"We will survive in style until they rescue us." Lorraine laughed, applying her lipstick. Both of us smelt rank, but attempting to look healthy and well felt humane.

"I'm parched after last night's beers," I told Lorraine, combing through my hair while minding my swollen elbow.

"It would be nice to have a sip of water. Clean water too," Lorraine emphasized. "If you really want to drink that bad, how about you go out and find some water for us?"

"I would go with a partner," I said. "I don't want to leave the premises of the S-440 alone. What if a rescue team comes and I miss it?"

"No hun, don't ask because I'm tired. But I think your plan is fantastic and I'll support you," she said. *I wish Cort were here to trash talk her with me*, I thought wistfully.

"If a rescue team came, I would hope that you would still wait for me," I said.

"Honey, I'm trying to get out of here." Lorraine scratched her head. "I hate lice. I hate bugs. I hate nature. I don't want to be here. I want to sue; I want a life and to get back to my kids." Lorraine bent down, plucking a yellow flower and handing it to me in a patronizing manner. "We can eat plants for water if need be. I'll be hibernating."

The safe move, Ary, is for you to stay near the S-440, Cort would have told me.

Frustrated by Lorraine, I told Lucas of my vague plans to venture away from the S-440 in hopes of finding at least water with the help of a partner. Lucas egged on my adventure.

"How are you thinking of getting back here?" Lucas asked.

"I haven't thought of that." I shied away from the question. "I was hoping to not go on my own."

"Your idea sounds great. I'm not strong enough to go anywhere, but it would be a stupid tactic for you to get lost in the woods," he said. "If you are set on leaving, let's come up with a plan for how you're going to track your route. Otherwise, you should stay here."

The plan we came up with was to collect random objects from the S-440 and to leave a trail of them behind. Lucas jokingly called this Operation Hansel and Gretel (otherwise known as operation HG).

"Promise me that if a rescue team comes you will wait for me," I begged him. Lucas saluted me mockingly.

"Roger."

I went into the unknown surrounding the S-440 with my swollen arm in a sling and a bag full of miscellaneous items belonging to the S-440. In my pockets I carried a long rope, three empty water flasks, and a flashlight. The first item I left to hang off a tree branch was Lucas's belt.

The thicket of scratchy weed plants clung on to my flight suit's pant legs. Tiny bugs whined into my ears and persisted in their drone. I could smell the sweat on myself and felt the puddles of fear pooling under my armpits. I turned a distance and, with difficulty, tied a wrapper on top of a bush.

A whisp tickled my shoulder. I scratched at it and with horror realized that I had crushed a black spider. I let out a whimper upon seeing the dark hemolymph trickling down from the thumb-sized spider. Unreasonable fear followed me from any slight touch or tickle thereafter.

There was no easy path around the woods. I was surrounded by parades of well-established trees, but I kept my focus on the ground, overstepping roots and picking easier paths. Branches cracked under my boots, each crack causing me to pause. My heart was beating a nauseating rhythm. I tried to breathe through the heightened sensations.

I left behind a manual on the EKG machine. I took steps to the next tree and felt something disgustingly sticky on my face. The air was becoming so hot and stuffy too. I unzipped the upper half of my suit to my midriff just for some ventilation. I screamed, wiping the cobweb off my face. I whimpered and felt panic rising. Then I looked at the threads plastered on my right hand and laughed.

I couldn't explain it. I could laugh as loud as I wanted. How does one end up like I have, in the middle of a dense forest, leaving behind trash to find their way back to a crashed helicopter? But it didn't matter what kind of trashy plan that I had. I felt determined that if this was the way to survive, so be it. *This was a new Ary.*

I continued surveying the land, leaving behind a guide of protocols, an empty metal can of triple espresso coffee, and miscellaneous wires. At some point, the thicket cleared out and a clay road appeared. I could follow along this straight path, but I was unsure what to make of it. I walked along the clay path on the grassy side until I came upon a set of boot prints.

"What on earth?" I murmured to myself. The footprints kept leading on in the clay path. The prints faltered from time to time, but I realized that the clay road was also leading to a clearing with a lighter gradient of light.

Is it dumb to follow foot tracks? No idea. It's a shame there is no Cort to advise.

They could belong to the remnants of my civilization here. Or it could be unknown strangers of the other world. They are the extraterrestrials that have no place in our society.

I could start to hear a different type of acoustic in addition to my trampling of weeds and rustle of trees. The vibration was low and rumbling. It could be a mill. A generator? An aircraft?

I trailed around the seemingly never-ending clay path. More light filtered in through the above canopy and suddenly widened into a beautiful view of a river. The clearing was long and had coffee-colored sand with clunky cuts of rocks. On the opposite side of the pool of water were steep hills and families of trees.

I sat on a deformed, jagged rock to remove my boots and peeled off the sweaty socks. I approached the shore as it gently licked my feet in greeting. Cupping my hand, I tasted the water. It was so cold! I giggled from the surprise. Would I get diarrhea? I didn't know! But I took one handful, then two, and then I filled a canteen to drink with ease. I watched the empty bottles gulp the water down.

I sighed in relief, feeling even my hunger cues being dulled by water.

Satiated, I filled the two-gallon canteens I had on me. I basked in the glow of the mirror that glittered at me with a hopeful light. I had become used to the textures of the canopy trees and dull bark, but I was surprised at how flat the water appeared to be. It was a mirror that glittered at me with hopeful light.

Setting aside the canteens, I decided that the chance was ripe to take a bath.

I took off my suit and undergarments and tried out the water a second time. The water was cold, and I shivered while trying it out on my bare shins. After a minute, I gritted my teeth and lowered the rest of my body into the water. While sitting on the river floor, the water rushed over my knees to form the silhouette of a water dragon.

My body was broken up by light and appeared yellow in the water to me. I realized that I had no idea how I looked anymore. Of my face, I could only see the hint of a nose, which the eyes naturally ignore. I had no idea if the beauty on my face would have any merit on matching apps. Those matching apps like to match people of similar attraction to each other and occasionally will try their fate at matching "out-of-league" potential mates.

I laughed at the strange thought that was kilometers away from me.

It felt sacred to bathe in the water. I laid down in the shallow water, letting the river mess with my hair and roll it this way and that way. And when I had enough, I stood up and let myself dry in the sun, shivering with delight as I watched my skin prickle up in attempts to keep me comfortable. With difficulty, I clambered into my suit and unstrapped my boots to ease in my feet.

I followed back through the clay road. Life in New Khan was like how a sleeping child is led by a hand. But in the woods, there was no safety or guidance to help me home.

Eventually the path faded, and I started finding my rubbish. I decided to leave the path of rubbish I made in case of future trips, but I couldn't seem to find the EKG manual I had placed near the S-440. The outline of the S-440's blades appeared at a distance, and as I approached our new base, I thought, *This crash wasn't that scary. Maybe this will be a short adventure that I'll be able to look back on fondly someday.*

CHAPTER 7

IN THE EYE

Despite having freshly washed myself, my hair was clumping back by my sweat. In the sweltering heat of the afternoon sun, Lucas and Lorraine chose to lie in the shade outside of the S-440, the opened drug medication box beside them and in use. Lorraine was on her side, cupping her hand while Lucas ranted animatedly. The appearance of water raised their excitement like plants sprouting out of a germinating seed. For the first time, the water I had gathered was met with praise from my coworkers; it felt more delicious than drinking the water itself. Their praise was enough to make me forget about my swollen arm or the blisters at my heel.

"This is amazing," Lucas groaned, pouring the canister over his sweat-speckled forehead. "This should be enough until we are rescued." I couldn't help but smile, wishing Cort were here to revel in my newly found popularity.

"I, too, have good news," Lorraine said coolly. "It was too hot for me to sleep, and I was forced out of bed. Well, I walked for a little bit until I saw an apple blossom with delicious fruit. I was talking to Lucas about this because I'm too old to climb those trees. We figured we could use some of your young muscle to get up there." She grinned at me.

"Did you try it? Did it taste any good?" I asked as a way to delay her demand. I liked feeling like a hero and wanted to keep my high praise.

"It was fine. It has a peachy flavor. It's juicy and has water."

"Huzzah for no more grubby dandelion salad," Lucas said. "Lorraine was even joking about eating them bugs. Go forage some apples with her, eh?"

"I'm rather tired after all of that walking," I said, heaving myself and the bag onto the grass. "And my arm has been swollen."

"Please, we'll be rescued at any moment," Lorraine squealed. "Let's have a small adventure before we leave. I'll give you some morphine if you'd like."

These adventures take up more energy than these people realize, I grumbled to myself.

I delayed the so-called adventure by mentioning the boot tracks I had seen along the clay road. "What do you think?" I asked Lucas directly, probing for a response. Lucas tended to hide his facial expressions, which became even more difficult to decipher with his bushy gray beard growing unkempt.

"These tracks can't belong to anyone from our civilization, because it's too far away from the outskirts," Lucas said slowly. "And they're not stupid because they led you to a source of water. I'm not sure, but it's comparable to that video game—*Lost*, I think it was called?"

"What if they were outsiders?" I asked.

When I was younger, there was a special documentary report on outside inhabitants. The reporter, with her properly styled hair, looked out of place compared to the simple, sullied female guide. The woman's hair was styled in two loops of glossy braids, and her austere face made her look inhuman. The female guide pointed to the sheep and the reporter guessed at the significance, showcasing how their morals were based on century-old traditions to cause suffering on animals. Because I was a child, the images of overturned cattle hanging upside down from trees followed me into nightmares.

"I don't know much of them, but I do know that they would hardly be able to tie a knot," Lorraine said, clutching at her stomach. "I'm getting a slight stomachache. Either the water is twisted with pathogens or I'm starving."

I heaved a sigh, undoing my damp boots to dry and picking at my blisters. "Are you coming with us, Lucas?"

"I'm working on something special," he said, shaking his head with mystery. Lorraine laughed mockingly at him.

"He's just sleeping all day."

"No, you'll see," he said with defiance.

The trek was quiet. I felt irritated in the heat of the daytime, bending away from stooping tree branches, every heel strike digging into my blisters. Lorraine began the hike in a pleasant mood and would occasionally pause to pant by a tree.

"Oh, I don't feel so good," she gasped, bending over.

"How about we go back?" I said after Lorraine paused once more by an oak tree to heave.

At once, I felt an uncomfortable presence nipping at my skin. A red bug was snaking along Lorraine's poufy hair as she retched onto a trunk. "There's a bug in your hair," I said, picking through her curls as the bug slipped away from my grasp. I patted at the dry cloud of hair again when the bug disappeared. *How strange*, I thought.

I cranked my neck to look up in the exact opposite direction in the sky to see the source of the red laser pointer. It was a pair of lasers, or a pair of pupils, straining to identify us.

They were flying in from above. A shadow of a wing passed over us. Two red laser eyes stared at us with rage, and a terrible shriek shook leaves close by off of the trees. It was a bird with metallic joints. A deep instinct broke through my waning high, begging me to run.

"We need to go." Despite my instincts, I shook in place, rooted to the ground. This was terrifying. Lorraine had not yet registered the presence of the metallic hawk; she was sick or high or an unfortunate combination of both. I kept my eyes on the creature as it clenched its claws midair, almost like it was charging itself for a potential collision. The euphoria of my painkillers abated in the face of whatever this gruesome creature was.

I pulled Lorraine down into a defensive curl as a shot blasted beside us. The bird's beak tumbled like a released crossbow arrow into the nearby oak. I screamed and cried at the same time, but the crash covered the noise.

Having recognized that it missed its target, the metallic hawk used the force of its clawed legs to pull itself out of the hole. It shrieked with fury at the audacity of missing. This was the buffer that saved me.

"Get up!" I yelled at Lorraine's rolling eyes, and then rubbed her sternum. She hissed and groaned, but it was now easier to pull her weight upward. Springing to my feet and throwing her arm behind my neck, I dragged her along behind me.

I threw one foot after the other mechanically. The blisters on my heels burst into open wounds. My tears had blurred my vision to the point where all I saw was a blur of chestnut-brown bark and tree. Leaves slapped my face eagerly.

Up above, a second differently pitched shriek resounded. I looked up to see a smaller metallic hawk circling up above.

Focus forward! Faster, go faster!

My heart was banging wildly. I could hardly breathe; I was drowning in panic. *I can't do this—I can't—what is going on?*

I looked up just in time to see the second metallic hawk clutching at its claws in midair. I whisked Lorraine to the side as the creature blasted its beak into the ground. Both of us wailed again while curling into a fetal position. I covered my ringing ears with my hands.

Lorraine woke up enough to stumble in her own weight. This time, after springing to our feet, we linked arms. Finally, a sprint was possible. Despite the lengthy period when the first hawk recognized it had missed and pulled out its beak, both metallic hawks were regaining on us. The larger one soared above the canopies, its brown wings cunningly reflecting light. The smaller metallic hawk was riding through the canopy, following behind us closer to the ground.

Suddenly, Lorraine's linked arm fell loose. She had landed on her knees behind me. I could hardly stop myself from falling abruptly.

"My stomach!" Lorraine gasped, clutching at her right side, fighting for breath. I could see the land-riding metallic hawk closing in on us.

There was a rock the size of a heart at my feet.

With all the might I had learned from playing fitness video games, I hurled the rock at the center of the perfectly angled face. *It's one shot.* In slow motion, I saw the rock twirl in the air. The curve of the rock's path could have easily missed my target.

It landed on an eye. The metallic hawk closed its eyes, shook its head in confusion and flailed its speckled feathers. The moment was ripe.

I jerked Lorraine back up on her feet. My own feet burned. My chest hurt. Lorraine was not an easy partner to carry.

The sight of the S-440's blades beckoned me. My lovely S-440. *Go, go, go. Push, push.*

Lucas stood outside the S-440, baffled by the sight.

"In!" I yelled at him. This time, he was an obedient bastard.

I plunged Lorraine inside the scorching S-440 and then turned around to shut the back door, but the hinges refused to listen. Lucas understood the assignment and helped me pull the back door shut.

Lorraine keeled over, gagging clumps of dark green undigested food. I lay on the bench, struggling to catch my breath. For the rest of the night, we were like scared mice in a one-exit den. Out of the puny windows, the metallic hawks weren't visible. We didn't hear them either, but we didn't dare speak.

Lorraine looked horrible. She was shiny with sweat and becoming more confused as the night went on. I begged her to take small sips of water, all of which came back up into her bedpan. I couldn't tell what was wrong, but it seemed like the onset of digestive issues that were different from her motion sickness caused by the crash. Other than basic fluids, there was not much that I could do. And the worst thing was that I had already used most of the saline to liberally clean Lucas's burns; now, I was sticking Lorraine with microliters of saline.

Where was the rescue?

I was physically and mentally exhausted after the chase. A day had gone by without a comprehensive meal, and I had run the equivalent of a proper race against the metal hawks. I was tired of being ordered around, I was tired of being a caretaker, and I was oh so sleepy. . . .

The sticky heat lulled my eyes closed into visions of her dark vomit being carried along a river.

The following day, I woke up to Lucas shaking Lorraine's body. She was lying a little too still on the stretcher. I probed her, but her skin was cold, there was no pulse, and her muscles were rigid.

"Aye, Lorraine." Lucas slapped her face, but that was unnecessary. She was clearly dead.

Stunned and in disbelief, I turned away from Lucas and sobbed. *What was this cursed journey? Why was everything spinning out of control so quickly?*

As a nurse, I often see men crying only during catastrophic events, and Lucas was not an exception. He grieved openly with physical tears once we had dragged her body out into a ditch and respectfully crossed her arms over to make her look at peace. Even the sky cried out and started lightly drizzling. I picked some dandelions and lilac wildflowers to add some beauty to the fake grave while Lucas sang a mournful tune with a deep, comforting, baritone voice.

Oh, when I'll see you
We'll hike the mountains.
And soon I'll follow you back Home …

I deeply regret how my exhaustion had worn me down after the chase. Perhaps if I had fought my weariness harder, maybe I could have helped Lorraine more. But like Eve, Lorraine had bitten into the promising apple. I suppose that something in the apples she had eaten had not only been poisonous for the digestive system but dangerous for the heart. Without the proper technology and medications, I couldn't do anything. And even knowing that, I still felt guilty and thought that I needed to be punished, a feeling that would gnaw at me. Before her death, we were excited about the strange experience of living out in the woods. But Lorraine was the reminder to be cautious of our environment. Any creak or rustle alerted me. Any nourishment I put into my mouth I distrusted. Before her death, we had placed our hopes on a rescue. Now we were being singled out, one by one.

CHAPTER 8

PROMETHEUS AND THE HEROES

In writing this, Lorraine's death is still unpleasant for me to acknowledge to this day. Once her body was on a shallow scab in the earth, our minds had collectively switched to survival. Our hopeful optimism evaporated and sank into Lorraine's pseudo grave. We learned our lesson and staved off excess use of the drugs. We had to ration the pain medicine, after all.

The S-440 became our habitable industrial ruin with fickle temperature regulation. Once the sun's heat slicked off the aluminum, the S-440 became as cold as a refrigerator. We were lucky to morph ourselves into foiled cocoons in the nighttime using the emergency foil, but I needed a new goal. I was bored out of my mind, easily irritable, and needed something to think about or do since there was no Cort to entertain me.

I tried my hand at making a fire. All my attempts to grind the sticks harder or set up a structurally sound teepee were in vain. I was an idiot in this world because there was no Cort to tell me about the slim success of using damp sticks or how kindling and tinder are separate concepts.

"What is this silly fort you're building?" Lucas stood over me as I crouched over my structure. I told him about my new pastime.

"That's no way to start a fire," he snickered. I was ready to pounce on him to sew his trap up. He had already annoyed me with his gargantuan nighttime snore that kept me awake, fearing the metallic hawks would pick up the sound. But before I could do something, he disappeared to pull something out of the side of the S-440's compartment.

I turned back to my collapsing, "silly fort" when Lucas's footsteps warned me of his approach. He doused a brown oil over the collection of sticks. Then he lay down on his belly and flickered a spark out of a switch.

Nothing happened at first. One part of me wanted him to fail miserably for me to feel satisfaction. But the other half was excited for a new fountain of knowledge that was opening.

The sticks did eventually catch fire. The fire initially lay low and was hesitant to spread out, but with a few of Lucas's blows from his nasty thick lips, it was jovially dancing. Watching a fire spit out embers was about the most entertainment one could have in the woods.

Lucas sighed and heaved himself by the flames, setting the tub that had contained the brown oil far away from the fire.

"There was some potentially flammable oil to collect and use," Lucas explained. "Watch out and don't let the tub come near the fire, obviously. We can also cover it up with some stones or somin' to control it. If you want a fire," he warned, "you better watch out for it to not get out of hand. It would suck to burn after a shitty crash."

"Thank you, Mr. Prometheus," I said begrudgingly. "I didn't even know you had something to start a fire with. What else do you have?"

"Who's that?" Lucas dodged my question.

"Prometheus, the Greek myth about someone who brought fire to the humans and then suffered the wrath of the gods," I told him.

"Oh, my grandkids are into those stories," said Lucas. He reached around to pull out an earthy pair of mushrooms to knead onto a stick. "There's some VR world based off them, and the kids pick up all these weird stories about these one-eyed goblins."

"What are your grandkids like?" I asked, watching with entertainment how the mushrooms prickled and burned at the edges of their caps. Lucas perked up.

"They're crazy boys. Three of 'em. Lots of energy, but that works out for me. Actually, we were working on this VR game called *Oasis*. Heard of it?"

"Hm, no." I stretched out and lay on my back to stare at the clouds.

"It's this alternative environment where we build a world with whatever we find in that virtual, natural environment. It's an upgraded version of *Minecraft*, although you're too young to know that game."

I rolled my eyes playfully at his antagonism. "I bet you were part of that generation that had to complete VR addiction programs."

Lucas laughed. "Yeah, only because it affected my personal life. My wife, her name's Louisa, was all naggy back then. I went through it in the end." Lucas slowed down, picking at the gauze wrapped around his ring finger. "I do miss her."

I didn't say anything. I missed a lot too, but it was hard to say that I missed a specific person whom I could expect to see alive.

"I can't believe we are in this position," I said. "It was my first day on the job too."

"This tops the crashes I've been in," Lucas laughed.

"You've been in other crashes?"

"Yeah. Not quite in the wilderness, though, and I didn't get a single scratch. I was actually mighty lucky, 'cause my partner last time had a whole dozen cans of beer. We drank up the rig and waited till backup came. We had a jolly good time. Paul still expected me to keep workin'. I told him, 'bye-bye' and clocked out. He'll suck out your last juices if he has to."

"What do you think of Paul pushing us into this situation?" I asked. Suddenly, I recalled that Paul's glistening forehead frequently intruded on my dreams. I thought of bringing that up, but I was scared that Lucas would snap on me for having sided with Paul.

"He's an idiot. He couldn't give a crap about us. One time, I was dispatched to this hydroponic factory for a possible heart attack. No problem, we get there in no time and I approve all the coordinates. Big problem is that agricultural plots have dozens of these massive hydroponic factories."

"What's a hydra—phonic factory?" I asked.

"They're these big warehouses with fancy lights and growing greens and you have to run across a field to get from one building to the other. And meanwhile, Paul is yelling in my fucking ears that I need to focus on finding the victim. And I hate when someone gets all emotional in a stressful situation. It doesn't do any good."

"Glad that I didn't work long enough for Paul to yell at me," I mumbled sarcastically.

"Oh yeah. My partner starts pissing his pants from Paul chewing him out for being no good. Everyone is staring at us like we are crazies because we have a literal voice in our helmets telling us that we are a burden on the company. Finally found the right factory—patient had heartburn. Paul was pissed at me for not having the wrong coordinates that he gave anyway. My lord, can't wait to sue that sucker."

"He expected you to know where to go even with the wrong information?"

"Yes. He thinks so highly of himself and expects me to be the robot. But I'm no robot with internal GPS and mind reading. I'm a human. Here, try this." Lucas handed me a piping hot mushroom. I passed it between my hands to cool off. The mushroom tasted better than the crunchy, grubby insects Lucas had pestered me to try. Although the mushroom— which tasted like burned rubber—was nothing compared to food in NK City, it was appropriate for the time being.

I hadn't brought it up because of my inhibitions, but I decided to ask him the question that had been truly bothering me.

"Why did we crash, Lucas?"

"It's complicated. The visibility was down. My autopilot function performs the worst if the weather visibility is down to half a mile. I think that our tail must've hit a boulder—that was the first hit. It made us lose our balance entirely." Lucas sighed deeply. "Then it spiraled out of my control."

"How do you work with the autopilot function?" I asked, genuinely not having a clue.

"The autopilot system is a well-written program, no doubts about that. It's so easy to use that the freshly minted pilots coming out of school don't even know how to properly read gauges. But, especially with the dust storms that form from excessive heat, the program loses understanding of the altitude, the pressures, the surroundings. It's always a risk leaving an urban environment because we enter a climate that's unpredictable. I let the program run and I can man it but the damage on the tail made it beyond my control."

Lucas stopped abruptly and started shaking, rocking back and forth.

"I pride myself in being a professional. I really do. You know, I flew in the Air Force. I've flown through war zones, bombs, under bridges, whatever. You name it, I've flown through it and survived without making a costly mistake. But I can't stop rethinking what should have happened."

"I might've died if I had sat in Lorraine's seat," I shuddered.

"It's a twisted luck you got there."

"Is it really luck? It could have been a quick way out."

Lucas shook his head in disappointment.

"I had a really bad feeling that morning, but I'm used to ignoring fear. Fear stops us too often, but this time I hesitated. I didn't listen to my fear."

I stared at him, expecting him to continue. But he stared off into the ground with a meaningless look. Then he stared back at me with bloodshot, glassy eyes. "I am scared that we won't be found."

A bubble of anger rose within my chest.

"No, we will get back," I said with surprising determination. "I know you want to sue but think of Lorraine. She has a huge family who are worried sick about her. You'd know better, but it looks like she's the breadwinner of her family. And now their mother randomly disappeared? That's not fair, and they deserve to know what happened. Forget suing, that's just a side effect."

"You're a miserable romantic." Lucas sighed, and I tensed up for another insult. "I can appreciate that."

CHAPTER 9

HIGHLY PRICED EGGS

———

I fell asleep hungry that night, dreaming of our stale crackers growing into velvety cakes with vanilla frosting-cut mountains. The reality was that I was always hungry and the one appeasing thought that had been growing unconsciously in my head was now obvious by the hour. I wasn't eager to do it. I didn't want to break my own moral code. Killing another creature is against what New Khan stands for.

The next morning, I woke up to see Lucas again huddled by the fire fort. He was messing with some metal with a familiar look. On second glance, he was taking apart my sacred pearly earbuds—the key to my personal Cort. My blood instantly boiled, my heart skipped a beat, and my normal inhibitions and manners dissolved. Hungry Ary is different.

"What's that?" I demanded impatiently. "What are you doing?"

"Sorry Ary," he started. "I just need this part."

I heaved out an exasperated sigh. *How dare he touch my things?*

"What for?" I asked, worried. Lucas took his time answering, cradling the belongings.

"I remembered that there's a resistor in here that could use to replace the burnt out one in the radios. It's just an experiment, no promises that I'll get it to work."

One side of my brain hesitated in the confrontation and wanted to let the tension go. Having radios was a hopeful idea. But on the other hand, this confrontation was a culmination of the disrespect he showed me. I wanted to let Lucas know he had crossed my personal boundaries too often.

"Did you even consider asking me?" I stuttered. "Do you go through my stuff when I'm not around? You've been so secretive, what have you been hiding?" I folded my arms over, trying to control my shakiness and look confident. I had suspicion that Lucas nosed through my belongings, but to keep peace I decided to not say anything until now.

"I know how to work with these inside out. If we do ever get back into civilization, I'll fix it for you, no problem. And I'm not hiding anything." He showed the palms of his hands defensively. "I've been working on the radios to keep myself busy."

I remembered how my nurse mentors had spoken to me in intimidating tones that made me want to lick the floors of the hospital in hopes of making them happy. I mocked their tone of collected rage.

"Fix it for me now. It is too expensive to be out here in the woods."

"Ary, don't be stupid. I need it."

Lucas's fake gentle name calling stung. My chest tightened into a knot, and I felt heat rising through my cheeks. I left behind the strict tone.

"You're calling me stupid? I got you out of the S-440, I've been tending to your wounds, I'm the one who found us water, otherwise you'd be dead!"

"Of course, thank you." He mocked a gesture of piety like the saints on the stained-glass windows of tiny hospital chapels.

"But think about it. You're not in need of this right now. It's no use to you as a dead battery. I might be able to get us back online."

I felt my cheeks flush with heat. I stuttered over my words like how a one-year-old stumbles when learning to walk. "That's my stuff. I don't like that you touch it. I don't like how you don't care at all! Don't care about my feelings! Insult me like I'm nobody. You never consider what I would think. You might as well just die on your own out here."

I turned around on my heels and blew out an anxious breath.

"Where are you going?"

"Me? Well, 'stupid' is going to figure out how else to survive. Hope you have a great time going through other people's belongings!"

"Aye, don't be like that!" Lucas yelled after me. I was mildly relieved that he could only hobble meagerly. I picked up my bag, miscellaneous tubs clanging inside, and slung it over my shoulder.

I was boiling with anger, but I also secretly wished that I hadn't argued with Lucas so that we could discuss my plan to get food. While he loved to insult, he had helped me with my plans for finding water last time. On the other hand, I felt better yelling at him. I was not an emotionless rock; I would not tolerate any more insults!

And then I would consider what his reasoning was and wonder if I was in the wrong. Then I'd rethink our conversation—because it felt amazing putting him in his place—and repeat the same cycle of thinking.

Lucas would probably keep running over me if I didn't say no, I thought. *I'm right. He wouldn't share his food rations until Lorraine had begged him, but he has no boundaries when it comes to other people's belongings.*

I followed along my usual path of rubbish to find the river, which had become part of my daily walk to collect water to bring back. Out of fear for the metallic hawks, I kept myself hidden under the trees and avoided the clearings, scared to even bathe in the water for fear of an attack. I passed the familiar rotting log, the never-ending oaks, and various bushes. While I had been scared of this path before, I felt comfortable and even fond of the trail that led to the river—a familiar friend to me that I was proud to know. *I'm not useless.*

My vague plan was to see if I could bait the fish I had seen in the river. My ideas involved finding a long enough stick to needle a bug on as bait. After that, I could try sticking in a tiny pocketknife—the size of a nail file—to catch the fish in its tracks. I found a lengthy stick with a dull point on the end, which was the easy part.

For a moment, I wished I could have found some guidance from Lucas. This plan was not so well thought out. Finding bait would be harder, not just in principle, but also because I despise bugs.

Some of the bugs I found were too small, while other flying ones were difficult to catch. I was also becoming angrier with every step, not just from arguing with Lucas, but from the difficulty of the task, heat fatigue, and hunger.

Bugs tend to hide under tight spaces.

I crouched onto the forest floor and flipped over a shale rock piece where I found a variety of bugs: fat, black, emerald green, huge pincers, small antennas. I cringed looking at them and had a heavy desire to quit. I'd make the trip quick and apologize to Lucas. I noticed a pattern of stripes slither in the shadow of a bush.

I shrieked. It slithered to reveal itself bigger and longer. It was a maroon-patterned snake, its beady black eyes glaring at me. I stumbled back away from the bush, stupidly waving my stick at the snake. It hissed menacingly at me while showing off her pink mouth with her claw-like fangs.

I had two options. I could leave the snake alone, or I could try throwing a pocketknife at her in an attempt to kill her. Would that be silly to leave myself weaponless?

I stayed put and the snake didn't intend to approach me. I raised myself on my tiptoes and saw a mound of white balls stacked on top of each other. They were eggs, all sticking to each other like balls of clay. The snake hissed at me, clearly upset that I had spotted her most prized possessions. They were the equivalent of my treasured Cort.

I would be an idiot if I didn't take advantage of this situation, I thought. *There's her and then there are the eggs. I couldn't kill a thing! Or can I?*

I glanced at the forest floor and remembered the heavy shale rock I had examined. *If I use the rock, I obviously have only one turn with it. I'd have to aim it so that it won't crush the eggs.*

She hissed at me again. I fumbled around with the stick, coaxing her to move a little bit. She was obviously not happy and quivered around my poking threats. About three-quarters of her body was still covering the eggs. I jabbed at her some more, still keeping my distance. All my movements were erratic and fueled with adrenaline.

Her head started closer to my feet, randomly popping up and down. I stooped to the ground, picked up the shale and threw it onto her head.

Did I kill it?

The rock had landed square on the head, the bodily juices seeping out into a nasty pool. I took a step closer to investigate, but her body wriggled around like she was having a seizure. I jumped back and squealed. *She seems alive!* I waved my stick as if I was about to fence the snake.

Despite her squirming, she was weighed down by the rock. I couldn't see her head, but splotches of her blood had sprayed out. I was confident that the damage was done. I felt horrified at what I had done and looked away to find a rock to gather my breath and observe if she was dead.

Two meters away from our battlefield, I noticed she had lain twelve eggs. I marveled at them, surprised that such a slim creature could put out such beautifully round eggs. I took note that I would need to collect them.

After a few minutes, she stopped writhing as much. I thought that the practical solution would be to collect her body to roast on the fire. After finding a matching stick, I tried to pull out her body from under the rocks with long enough sticks that would keep her at a distance away from me. That was a mistake, because she was not dead by the sound of her poisonous fangs—thankfully, I had not removed the heavy load on her coiling body.

Then I considered cutting off parts of her meat and tail. By putting my own body weight on the opposite side of the rock, I realized it was much easier to cut her, which was absolutely disgusting. I whimpered the whole time, but another side of me thought being able to harvest my prize was mildly satisfying. Nevertheless, the snake eggs were still left. I sidestepped the remnants of the mother's angry body and collected the blood sprayed eggs into a spare bedpan. The deed was done.

~

On the path back to the S-440, I saw one footprint. Then another one. I bent down to gingerly pad along the length of it, and the clay gave in easily. It had a strong indent going forward, as if whoever left this mark was on a mission that had to be completed immediately. There was another foot-mark of a different size, and maybe a third or a fourth. And they kept coming closer and closer to the S-440. I passed the wrapper in my garbage trail and felt my heart speed up.

This must be the rescue coming for us. Only four days had passed—they couldn't have just forgotten us! Lucas and I had dreamed of how the rescue mission would take place. It could be by helicopter. There could be multitudes of volunteers scouring the woods for a hint of our presence.

I finally reached the S-440, but it did not look like itself anymore. It was chaotic. The tidiness Lorraine and I had restored was scrambled with the campfire trampled on with great fury, not only by bootsteps, but also the rain that had slit the fire's throat.

"Lucas," I called, feeling the tension in my chest rise. Was this some sort of sick prank?

Rescue could have come for us, but was Lucas one to leave behind comrades? Had I missed my shot on being rescued? I did not want to miss the comfort of returning to society.

"Stupid, stupid, stupid!" I yelled. "I don't even need food!" I kicked the empty tank. There must have been no point in going out for food. All useless.

The rain was putting full force on, as if some angry force decided to turn the knob of strength on me.

I stumbled to the inside of the S-440's ruins and set my fresh food to the side. The cabinets had been opened and ruffled through. The monitors and the expensive machines were gone. Glass, metal, screws, microchips, and wrappers were scattered everywhere. The locks for the special cabinets had been tampered with. Mud streaked throughout the cabin. Footprints were smeared on the gray floor.

Nothing made sense in the chaos. Was I seriously left behind for the dead? Of course the argument had happened, but Lucas's obstinate personality didn't come across as malicious or vengeful to this degree.

If Lucas had been rescued, he would have taken his belongings. I know that he had prized possessions stored in his backpack that he was extremely protective of, to the point that he suggested we lock away our belongings. I had agreed to hide them away simply because of the bug infestations that plagued the S-440. I applied my finger to the sensor and upon opening found all three backpacks: mine, Lucas's, and Lo's. Lucas's dirty blue backpack was slumped over Lo's empty deflated bag.

Lucas's most prized possessions were in the bag, items that I would think he'd take if a rescue team had come for him. There was an out-of-battery portable screen typically used for engineering designs. It looked old and scratched, but it would make sense that he was protective of old technology that's more sensitive to water and moisture. A thin, square leather wallet lay next to the bag, with a couple of plastic cards including his pilot license and the keycard to his aircraft. Wallets were slowly fading out of fashion since currency had become digital, but I assumed that Lucas carried around the wallet like an off-duty knight would carry his silver armor. On one side of the wallet was a picture of Lucas and his wife posed in humble attire, his arms encircling her torso. Lucas had also clearly been hiding stale bread that he was unwilling to share with me. I swallowed too big of a bite into my mouth, then shoved the plastic wrapping into my pocket for later snacking.

"This is strange," I said out loud to no one. "Was Lucas even rescued?"

I stepped outside to circle around the S-440 and quickly spotted footprints leading out of the aircraft. The tracks were leading in the exact opposite direction of the path to the lake. I hesitated, taking in deep breaths and feeling tense with every new finding.

A sturdy tree branch lay in the shadow of the S-440. I fished out the pocketknife from my sling bag and stuck it into an appropriate pocket. *Better to have even a small weapon in case I'm jumped.* The rainy clouds had also dimmed my visual surroundings. Buried somewhere in the bench of one of the cabin's seats, I found a large portable flashlight to sling over my neck.

I crept along one footprint to the next set and onto the next set. I called out Lucas's name to no avail. The grass and overgrowth covered the prints, so I'd take my tree branch to shift the grass to find another one. Panicking that I lost sight of the tracks, I feverishly shined my light one way and the other way. The prints were faint, as if they had taken off at a gracious running speed.

The wind picked up, and I regretted having cut off the sleeves of the suit. I shivered and zipped up what I could while the rain flooded the ground, erasing the staggered boot prints. My own boots soaked up the rain like plastic buckets. The hard rain pellets flickered the light of the flashlight back to me.

A shadow danced in the bushes. My heart sped up.

"Who is it?" I swallowed hard, raising my lone tree branch and angling my flashlight toward the dark. "Show yourself."

An ordinary bird cackled at me in the tree behind me. I whirled around the opposite way. Then faced back the other way. I approached the dark veil of bushes to find nothing. The weight of the rain was pulling me down and I was uncontrollably shivering from my heightened emotions.

"I hate this," I said out loud to no one. "I could've sworn—"

I backed up, giving up on following the tracks. These were not the right conditions to track down Lucas. With heightened vigilance, I carefully made it back to the S-440 drenched and shivering to the bone. I set my travel bag to my side, placing the thick tree branch on top for safety measures. *I'll find a nice metal rod to replace that as a weapon*, I thought to myself.

It'll be another weapon to keep handy.

I wanted to cry. I wanted to eat. I wanted to sleep. I wanted words of comfort. I wanted to feel warmth. In addition to my weak condition, the questionable surrounding wildlife, and my disconnect from society, perhaps I had missed my opportunity to leave. Or maybe not. My clouded mind could not make sense of all the hints left behind. But regardless, I knew that without Lucas's support, any other mistake would mean that I would be left for dead.

The rain had not subsided, and the easiest thing to do was to crawl into a cocoon of a thermal blanket and sleep. I activated and shoved hot packs into my metallic cocoon and sank into darkness to the meditative pitter patter of the rain the mold bred on.

I slept for an impossible amount of time, but I could tell that it was daytime since the sun was almost in the center of the sky. I woke up thinking I had the most comforting dream that night, and it was slipping out of my memory. I lay in my cocoon, staring at the gray ceiling of the S-440.

I stretched and crawled down into the bath of sunshine outside of the S-440. Between the chilling air and my warming flight suit, my skin prickled up in delight of the warmth.

I fished out my bins with eggs and pieces of snake, wrinkling my nose at the smell. Unfortunately, the exact same smell that was unattractive to me was attractive to pesky little flies. The snake meat needed to be roasted.

I had seen Lucas setting up fire with the flammable oil that he had, and like a child I tried to imitate when I had seen him do it. Stepping over the junk left behind, I found the lighter that he used and shook off the excess water. The leak of flammable oil was somewhere off to the right of the cabin, and I salvaged some more into a small urinal. I poured it onto the older set of oil and flicked the lighter. First spark and nothing happened. Second spark and nothing happened. Only by the fifth attempt was a tiny spark emitted, and the oil magically grew into a tall flame.

Now I needed to fry the snake before too many of the flies ate away my prize. In children's books, there's a neat setup with two pieces of U-shaped branches holding the meat over the fire. Unfortunately, fairy tales aren't always true to real life. I made up my mind to put the snake on a slab of metal from the S-440 to imitate a frying pan.

I did not want to touch the snake at all, but I was aching with hunger. I wasn't even curious what it looked like yesterday because I could already see the pool of blood it was marinating in. It was disgusting and morbid, but I didn't want it to go to waste. I hesitated several times before I mustered the courage to open the container the snake was in and throw it onto the metal scrap, pouring water on top as a safety measure. I found a piece from a knocked-off blade and turned the snake on its sides.

The snake turned out burnt, tasteless, and far from a luxurious meal. Biting into the meat and clattering my teeth against the snake's vertebrae was odd because it reminded me how I achieved this prize in the first place. But then it reminded me of sharing meals of salmon with my mother when I was younger. I had been disturbed to skin the salmon's scales and would become genuinely upset if a spare bone popped in my mouth. My mother would sigh and pick apart the salmon's meat to get rid of the bones, and then she'd slide my plate back to me.

Not having anyone, even Lucas, to share this meal with was disappointing. Lucas would not have said anything, but I know he would have appreciated the meal. Maybe he would have complimented me again.

When I finished eating the snake, I felt full for once. However, this had had no effect on my satisfaction. There was no one to laud me and no one to share a meal with.

CHAPTER 10

PREY AND PREDATORS

On the first day without Lucas, I woke up because of how itchy my face was. There were patches of swollen skin all along my forearms and thighs and shins because I had left the S-440's back door open, and without a fire to ward them away, I was the new prey for the insects. I couldn't help but scratch the itches into open wounds that would later turn into scabs. NK City hardly had any bugs and, naturally, my body's immune system overreacted to any slight bug bite. *Must keep a fire overnight.* I noted to myself.

I practiced extra vigilance prior to the daily hike for water. My goals for the day were simple: to get the daily portion of water safely and to get enough water to try boiling the eggs.

How could I defend myself against wild animals? What if whoever kidnapped or killed Lucas came back for me? There were clunky pieces of metal from the S-440 that I could swing around. I picked one up, swinging it one way and the other. Even handling something heavier than five pounds was exhausting. If only I managed to get back to society, life would be a breeze. I wouldn't have to rely on myself to calm down. At a click of Cort's button, nothing would concern me anymore.

"If only I could get back." I sighed out loud. Talking to myself like a madman was the best source of comfort. I enjoyed complaining to no one but the air. "I'm sick of being here, I'm sick of being gross and sweaty and then being miserably cold at night. My lips are chapped, my arm is still swollen, I have blisters all over my feet. And these rashes are killing me! Why did people ever like nature in the first place? Lying in a feather bed without bugs and mold and a thermostatic-controlled room is the dream."

A grumbling stomach and parched mouth were better motivators than fear—after all, it's instinct. The self-preserving tree branch was replaced by a durable yet light metallic rod from the S-440, tied around my waist using the excess fabric from the cut sleeves. My pockets were lined with ropes and the pocketknife or anything else I deemed mildly useful. Slightly more armed, I stopped procrastinating and conducted my usual daily trip to the river for more water. My vigilance paid off without any sightings of metallic hawks.

However, I did make a new friend when coming back to the S-440 when I spotted a set of glinting, golden eyes. They were bright, piercing, belonging to a fox. The long leaves of grass formed knife-ike shadows on the forest floor. The fox held my gaze, intent on holding eye contact with me. I froze, feeling the goosebumps standing up, and considered reaching for my sole protective piece of metal. I was frozen and so was she. I felt like I was staring at something familiar, like a reflective mirror.

I shifted weight from one foot to the other. Immediately the tension between us relaxed. The fox slunk a dark paw closer to me out of its camouflaging bush. She had a surprisingly huge head, black ears, and thin lanky body. I was in awe being so close to such a shy animal in the wild.

"You're so cute," I chirped to her softly.

I took some side steps around the fox's circumference, then went backward, seeing what would happen if I tried to escape the situation. The fox took two strange steps toward me, like it was dancing on its left hind leg. It reminded me of the protective gait patients with ankle fractures walk with. At the same time, the fox was bold enough to approach me even with her limping.

"This is normal for you?" I asked softly. I could have sworn the fox raised her head into a nod, then continued limping toward me.

"I would pity you, but you seem to be confident."

It doesn't matter to me, I imagined the fox telling me.

The moment was unexplainable, as if the fox and I had decided that we wouldn't cause any harm to the other. To her I may be tall, but I was not leaping to attack her. She seemed wise, choosing her own battles.

The fox stopped a meter in front of me. I crouched down, offering her to smell my fingers. I could tell she was not keen on smelling me. She still wanted to keep the boundary of the wild in her.

"I respect that." I told her, relaxing my hand and pulling away from her. "We're the same. Just some rogue survivors. I should take lessons from you. Raise me like a feral child, please?"

You're doing okay, I imagined her saying to me.

"Want to come with me?" I asked her. To test her willingness, I turned around as if to leave but kept my head swiveled back to her. I took a few steps and felt disappointed that she didn't follow. Her dark ears were drawn back quizzically. I understood the message.

"Goodbye friend," I whispered softly. With full souls, we parted ways to continue our searches.

Meeting the fox rejuvenated me; it was the first time that I had met a different species from myself that wasn't trying to hurt me. In fact, if anyone could have caused harm, it was me. I was the one who could have beat the poor fox into becoming my dinner, or in my weakened state at least have given the fox another disability. But I wouldn't do that. Maybe it was my delusional mind reflecting on silly thoughts, but I believed that my new canine friend and I were too similar.

I didn't know how to cook, especially boil eggs, but throwing them into hot water seemed about right. Once I started the fire the way that Lucas taught me, I added a metal canister on top to stir the eggs on.

I remembered the beauty of my own diet back in civilization. No animal was hurt by my decisions. I could eat all the truffles I wanted. Food was made specifically for my taste buds while being perfectly tender and sweet.

But looking at the swirling snake eggs, I realized that I didn't feel much remorse anymore. I was proud that I thought quickly enough when fighting the snake. That string of events could have made me as dead as Lucas. In society, it was morally wrong to kill or harm animals. Was I now a bad person?

One of the snake eggs had cracked and the liquid protein was cooking in the boiling water.

"What to do?" I asked out loud to the canister. *Bubble, bubble.* The water gurgled back at me with apathy.

In one quick swipe, I knocked the canister off the fire and let the hot water spill over. Out came the cracked egg with its cooked protein tail, and then the other small egg that I had managed to sneak into the small lip.

I cracked the intact egg open. It hadn't cooked at all! It spilled its yolk all over my swollen, patchy hands.

"No, no, no," I mumbled to myself, sucking the yolk off of my hands like a child licking off the chocolate frosting. But the yolk kept running away from my tongue, dripping onto the grass. Letting my prize run away to leave a path of sticky foamy fingers was frustrating.

The second cracked egg with the protein tail was, to my surprise, properly cooked. I gobbled it up like a gremlin.

Afterward, I began sorting and organizing the S-440's mess. My idea was to count the inventory and see what was still intact. The drug box was gone. The computer was gone, and so were the monitor, the ultrasound, and the robot CPR. I gave up trying to figure out what was missing. Lying in my sweaty undergarments, I stretched my arms out on the bed. I thought I heard an unusual crackling noise.

I snapped up, fingering for my protective piece of metal junk that I had put away.

"That sound is not normal," I mumbled out loud.

Another crackle. This time, it had come from deeper in the cabin. I approached the back corner of the cabin half naked—rod in hand.

Nothing happened.

I flicked the backpack to the side with my metal rod, my heart beating like crazy. Then I slowly peered under it. Then behind it. Something heavy was in there, something I didn't expect.

"A bomb?"

It was a square black box. There was a screen on it, an antenna, and some buttons.

It was an old-time radio, probably back from the early 2000s. This must have been the radio Lucas was working on when I left. I clicked on the power button, but the green dull screen taunted nothing back to me. Maybe it wasn't the radio that made a weird, wooshy noise.

I examined the radio like one would examine a meteorite. I pried open the back screen to reveal some old-time lithium batteries. I forced the rest of the radio apart, trying to string together what Lucas would have possibly been fixing. Electrical channels were connecting to one another through colorful lumps that looked like buildings on the green grid. *Far from my expertise.*

I examined the wires when I noticed that one wire was barely connected to a round attachment. I looped it to the round knob, but the wire fell off again as soon as I moved the radio slightly. I sat down to delicately maneuver the wire into a tighter ring. Only then did the screen light up to show me a combination of numbers.

"What is this?" I stared in disbelief. This was the only piece of equipment that actually worked. This could be my bridge into civilization. *Was this Lucas's doing?*

The radio was tuned to one wave, not transmitting a thing. Out of habit, I fixed it to two radio waves down.

"Help me," I transmitted, then sat back to wait. Not a peep.

"I was involved in a crash. Please help."

Nothing.

I lay in my cot, laying the radio gently over my stomach like a newborn child. Every so often, the wire fell off and the radio stopped turning on again. I would fix the wiring, then say something else into the radio: Who I was. What happened. What the S-440 looked like. About needing help.

The radio stayed hushed. The campfire I had set up outside was calming my nerves and made me feel warmer despite the nighttime cold by blowing in its crackling heat. I couldn't help but drift in and out of sleep, having brief fever dreams about someone replying on the radio but my mouth being paralyzed. I would wake up in cold sweat and then ease back into sleep.

CHAPTER 11

A QUICK ENDING

———

I was flying above a burning volcano—the hot, suffocating air blowing searing warmth into my face. I felt the blood on my face boiling. Lava angrily lulled around into a tumultuous river. It was stifling. I could hardly breathe.

I woke up smelling the volcano, and then I realized that it was not a volcano at all.

Most of what I could see was blinded by gray smoke, but the open backdoor showed the outline of a fire. Instinct fired up again.

I am getting out of here.

I felt along the walls of the S-440 for an exit. *That's the cabinet. I can't breathe. That's a square sign. Oh my god, this is it for me. That's a seat. That's a handle? No, it isn't. Yes, it is.*

Heart pumping, I kicked the hardly hinged side door open and stepped out to breathe in fresh air. I stooped over to gather my breath.

The fire was unbelievably loud. It popped, snapped, and hissed at me as if it were the snake's revenge. The campfire I had left overnight ravaged the surrounding trees and bushes and was quietly eating away the paint and metal below the S-440.

I have to save the S-440, I thought. It may seem like a stupid idea now, but I was rooted to the S-440. Where else was I supposed to sleep? How else would a stupid city girl like me survive?

My plan was to search the S-440's exterior compartments in the hopes of finding an extinguisher that I had no idea how to use. I touched the metal and yelped—it had absorbed heat from the fire—then blew off the heat from my fingertips as the tips swelled with pain. I pulled at the excess fabric on my suit to pry the damaged doors open. *A toolbox. Next compartment. A red rope. Here's what I need.*

I pulled the pin on the extinguisher and aimed at the root of the fire. To my frustration, my aim was in the opposite direction toward the sky. The flame menacingly sparked at me. I aimed the proper way this time. The first meeting of the fire and extinguisher resulted in gray clouds, and I turned away to blindly aim at my mighty target as I heard the extinguisher puff away at the enemy. The fire on the metal changed from a deep orange color into a subtle amber yellow. Then one tiny fire demon disappeared, leaving behind white putrid smoke.

But my extinguisher had no effect on the rest of the trees and flora surrounding the campsite, which were lit on fire. I sprayed the rest of the tiny extinguisher onto a nearby tree, and the yellow demon gave in this time. But I could feel the stream of white powder was depleting exponentially while the nearby oak tree danced in the wickedly orange fire. The extinguisher stopped releasing any of its white powder. I squeezed the handle harder, but to no result.

In a last attempt, I threw the empty red can into the fire. And then I ran. I heard behind me a small pop as the red can succumbed to the demon. I only saw snippets of what was happening because pausing and reflecting would have been a deadly delay. I ran and ran until I physically could not run anymore.

When I reflect and tell my story, I am also surprised that I survived that far. I could have died three times over. I did have the advantage of running marathons before. And being in nature forced me to learn new skills without the proper technique. But there also seemed to be that mysterious element of good luck that was following me around; I like to think of it as my mom's soul.

The fire escape sprint activated a debilitating cramp in my right abdomen, eventually causing me to fall onto my back in a star pose.

"I can see the sky." I coughed, staring upwards through the treetops. Heavy mucus thickened in the back of my throat.

Here I was with nowhere to go. My partner, as burdensome as he was, had disappeared. My temporary home, as crumbling as it was, had become an entrapment worthy of boiling an army. My hope resting on being found in the S-440 was meaningless. People talk about losing everything, but in that moment that was me.

After the burning of the S-440, I ambled around the trees for some time. I didn't dare come back to find it. I didn't want to. I was shocked at how everything I had known for comfort was disappearing and leaving me behind, naked. As for the S-440 burning, there was no one else to blame but myself. I had only wanted extra warmth and fewer bug bites, but I ended up with the exact opposite. I almost wished that I had stayed and burned in the S-440. Although painful, it would have been a much quicker death than hobbling around without a home.

A significant amount of time passed that was long enough to make me hungrier than usual. I would chew on grass blades for more than five times than habit would allow to "maximize the nutritional value." This would all make me nauseous, so I would lie on my back to ignore the discomfort and let the horrid feeling pass.

There wasn't much to recall other than draining fatigue. Knowing if I was dreaming or looking into darkness was impossible, and sometimes I thought I was being chased by horrid blue dots when closing my eyes.

Time has an uncanny way of shapeshifting. In New Khan, time was constantly running away like Cinderella at midnight. There was the daily career, there were trains to catch, there were Cort's reminders, there had been a mother to tend to, and there was my social time to balance. I had never sat down to stare into nothing until the crash in the woods. My mind felt like it had been switched from constantly being electrically pulsed by a vintage 1900s psychologist to a brain swimming in molasses.

But on the other hand, I had never since been in such a quiet place. Urban life is a constant alarming crow. How often are you aware of how loud your heartbeat is? Or of the quiet buzz in your ears? Sometimes the dead leaves would play a light percussion or desperate mating insects would string their bows. The forest was still, and I was ready to be buried in my meditation of it.

Admittedly, I became more careless and stopped searching for hiding spots. I was tired of being on the alert because I simply did not have the energy. At some point when I had turned over in my coffin of leaf padding, a familiar metallic rattle rang in the sky. It screeched the song of the metallic hawk as it launched itself into me.

I crouched into a defensive fold as the hawk's sharp beak struck into the ground. Dirt slapped my eyes. I let the momentum of the impact roll me away.

The hawk let out an ear-piercing screech, blinding me with its red laser eyes. Its talons grabbed my forearm, sinking in. I yelped and tried to press it away with my legs, but it moved with chilling determination to disarm me. I was a helpless ant stuck in a tin can.

I surrendered as the hawk clutched me into its flight. The wings rattled into full span as we gained height above the canopy.

I wasn't scared at this point. In fact, the flight was kind of fun. Looking below, there were the familiar clone copies of trees multiplied over and over. The metal hawk seemed to be flying me to see the gray scaly mountains in the distance. I was ready to see the worst.

The hawk howled with malice, steering me downward and toward the heart-dropping fall that I knew too well. It felt unsteady and unconfident, swinging me from side to side. Through the swarm of hair, I could see that the hawk's right wing was deforming from a hole in the feathers. The hawk was trying to compensate by flapping his wings with fervor. The hawk, and I as the captive, were heading straight into the ground.

This should be the quick end I had dreamed of.

CHAPTER 12

FROM HELL TO HEAVEN

Five dark muskets were glaring down at me. Behind them were five male owners of the guns.

I raised my palms defensively. "Please," I began. One man, with his face disguised under a filthy gambler hat and darkened eyeglasses, shouted something at me with a thick accent. I shook my head, hoping that was an international signal for not understanding. "I don't understand."

"Say you name!" He commanded sternly.

"My name is Aryana Hulagu," I whispered. "I don't have weapons. I was in a crash. I have been—"

"Are you transmitter?" The man asked, keeping himself at a distance. "What?" I croaked.

"Are you transmitter who call?" he repeated. I racked my brain for what that combination of words meant. Their dialect was unlike my own and not intelligible. He continued. "Crash? You know, use radio? Something like e-s forty?"

"I was in the S-440 crash," I stammered. *Was this my rescue?* "I was trying to reach anyone on the radio because we lost contact."

"Hm," said the strange spokesman. "We? Did city peoples send you?" He asked. I shook my head. "Are you look for city people? With computers?" He continued interrogating.

I fell into a monologue.

"No, I have no reason for being here," I told him, trying to show my earnestness. "I was in a helicopter crash and all of my crewmates died or disappeared. I'm trying to get back to my home. I don't have anything." I pulled out my pocketknife and threw it on the grass about three meters away from me, then turned over the other pockets to show them empty. "The people I knew are gone. My home is gone. Please help me," I begged.

The man's disguised face showed no apparent pity. *Did he even understand me?* He raised his hand, and I closed my eyes in expectation of pain.

"I'm sorry," the man said. I opened my eyes to see that all the muskets had been lowered. "We thought we heard you on radio, but we can never be too sure. We don't want spy."

"You heard me on the radio?" I was shocked.

"Hm," he hummed, and I couldn't tell if it was in affirmation or denial. He and the others slung the guns across their shoulders, then gave me a helping hand to stand up.

I thanked him. "What happened? One moment I was flying and now I'm here on the ground."

"Long story," said the man, taking off his glasses to show his thick black eyebrows and pointing to himself. "You call me Z. This is my crew. Sorry to scare you. We were looking for you after transmission, but helicopter was burnt. We thought you were dead by now."

"Wow," I said, breathless. "That's crazy."

"Okay girl," he cut me off. "Later story. We need to go to our boat because those birds will find us."

As we hiked toward the barge, Z spoke for the group and told me they had been tracking my trail from the S-440 after hearing my radio transmissions. They had no idea the metallic hawk that they shot down would be carrying the person they had been searching for, and they were just as shocked to meet a dead man like myself. Meanwhile, I was just as surprised that I had been rescued. I told Z a poorly strung tale about the crash, the fire, Lorraine dying, and Lucas's strange disappearance, all while occasionally biting back a tear. Although he didn't say anything, he listened to my crazy tale. Sometimes, he'd stop to ask me a clarifying question or click something at his crewmates in their common language. I figured he was translating a synopsis of my story to his crew, and I accompanied his translation by staring back at them.

~

Everyone imagines heaven a little bit differently. The Christians see it as a permanent escape from death and as an opportunity to worship God. Some see heaven as having all the material earthly possessions people dream of. Others see heaven as eternal sleep. I knew I was in heaven being on that ship. There was no tension or worry to bother me. I didn't have a care at all. Maybe that was my form of enlightenment.

And that was how I boarded the barge belonging to the savages of the woods who I could best describe as the "Metal Decomposers." The group rolled its boat through rivers and basins, hunting after the metallic hawks for what they considered precious metals. They collected old pieces of garbage in the rivers that were likely remnants from the city and broke down artillery into digestible pieces. Afterward, they would sell off the recyclables at sketchy black markets in New Khan or the neighboring settlement New Jochi.

Once a cabin had been cleared of its old storage to make space, I was guided past the captured Metal Hawk and the junk the barge carried. I thought I had seen something familiar from the S-440, but instead I saw broken and fixed radios alike, glinting colorful vinyls, rusted old brass trumpets, and odd machinery with gears that could turn. Z showed me into the cabin, which I familiarized myself with too well. There was no lock or handle on the door, only a physical hole to stick a finger into to push or pull the rotting door shut. Although the entrance was questionable, I liked the cabin itself. It was decorated with honey-colored oak, soft lighting, and rusted machinery from my world.

After my introduction to all the crew members, I spent the first few days lying seasick in my cabin. Having nothing to do, I would meditate on the wooden patterns on the ceiling; one panel of wood looked like two dark eyes with a slim nose in between them. Another panel of wood looked similar to the rushing wave patterns that I saw in the river I used to collect water in. Needless to say, I hardly interacted with the crew other than with its only woman, Baine, who would bring my meals. Baine and I were not able to have deep conversations because of language barriers, but she would ask me daily, "Okay?" and I would nod and tell her, "I'm okay."

I wasn't fed a lot, but at least I was fed. My guilty understanding was that all the crew had taken a ration hit to accommodate my needs. There were bland pickled vegetables and soft cheese, but the best food was the condensed milk with coffee. My digestive issues still followed, but I tried to keep my inability to keep the food down a secret from the rest of the crew.

After three reclusive days, Baine was fed up with my bash-fulness. Without speaking a common language, she pulled me up to the deck to interact with the crew.

I blinked hard from the unexpected sunlight and the reflecting waves. A series of harsh tongue clicks came from up above on the main mast by a ginormous, beer-bellied man with an astoundingly red nose and a poorly shaved beard. I didn't understand what he bellowed at his steering wheel, but it was clear that his language equated to a string of curse words. That was the leader of the ship, Captain Yank. One could find Captain Yank at the rudder with an ancient sonar in his hands, which he used to see if we were headed in the right direction. He would turn on the sonar and glare at the rotating circle. Then the apparatus would overheat and turn off. Captain Yank would curse in his language and wait another hour to turn it on again.

A furry being pounced at my stomach. It was the barge's resident dog with an unpronounceable name consisting of clicks that I simplified to My-Ra. Her face had a delicate, white mask to outline her eyes while the rest of her shaggy fur was chocolate brown. I pushed her away because of her awful smell, but she insisted on being friendly.

"How are you feeling?" Z asked me. "I hope you are not sick. Come play a card game with us."

"I'd love to," I said. Z handed the broom to me.

"First, a little sweep," he said with a mischievous look.

Even if it was far from the cleanliness I was used to, I appreciated the safety and comfort I felt. And as I picked up my energy once again, I was expected to contribute to the crew chores. If I left my cabin at the wrong time, I would be handed a simple chore like sweeping the floor or sorting through miscellaneous maps.

At first, I resented the sight of the broom being handed to me, but it was a fantastic opportunity to familiarize myself with the crew. No one else spoke my language, but I joked with Captain Yank's son—a teenage age sailor named Jerimiem, with a distinct red scar on the right side of cheek, who was expected to take over his father's position for maritime matters. Although this respectable expectation hung over his head, the only activity on the boat that Jerimiem enjoyed most was playing with My-Ra the water dog.

Baine was Captain Yank's daughter, but she could easily pass as a male because of her bluntly cut hair and rough way of speaking her language. Captain Yank also tried to teach her navigational skills in the sea and, although she feigned interest, Z told me, "Baine good hunter. She has good eyeballs and young strength."

There was also the keen-eyed Shering, the maritime engineer. From my understanding, he and Z worked together to assess valuable metals, what would sell in the market, and how to take apart any machine and restore it. We didn't bond that well at all because he was a shy man.

In the evening, I would be greeted with bitter, fermented, homemade beer. When the boat was headed in the right direction, the crew would sit down for a simple gambling game that I learned only through watching previous matches. The sailors were well versed in the game and kept leaving me with losses. In fact, it became a running joke for me to cover my eyes and mockingly cry to foreshadow the losses I would have.

In one match, I knew that luck was on my side. My heart beat a little faster and, for a brief second, self-doubting thoughts flooded in. *How would they react if I won?*

Then I realized how silly those thoughts were. I could have easily been killed by them four days ago—what was there to worry about now? When it was my turn to reveal my cards, I confidently teased the cards out onto the table. Captain Yank looked at me with intimidating, stern eyes. And then he laughed gruffly, slapping my back.

"Good!" He coughed, passing me his pipe of tobacco. In NK City, the cough would have steered me away from taking the pipe, but I accepted the graciousness of the action and laughed.

On the last day of our journey, the lethargy was finally starting to subside, and I left my tight cabin on my own accord for a walk on the deck to greet the northeastern wind. The hull creaked as the icy cold water churned out waves from under.

I was used to the sour, dank reek of the water. As Z told me, we had traveled away from the brackish river and were traveling to their settlement port. Graceful white herons stood at the brink of the shore. Oyster farms lined the outskirts.

"Almost home," Z said, spooking me from behind as I pet My-Ra. "You meet my girl G. She sing good."

"She's musical?" I asked, unsure what her name really was. "That's rare where I'm from."

"Maybe for you." Z shrugged his shoulders and pointed toward the heap of coal and shovels. "Help me move."

CHAPTER 13

WARS, CRIME, AND OGEDEI

———

The Metal Decomposers' settlement was not even the size of a town; it consisted of about six different families that added to a total population count under one hundred. The settlement's name was unpronounceable to me because of an emphasizing click on the "o," but it was best anglicized to Ogedei. The morning was foggy and cool, but I could still see it lacked the symmetry and patterns of New Khan's repetitive skyscrapers. This civilization was a loose collection of junk slapped together with the geometric buildings lying low to the ground. A hesitant rainfall had come and left an oxidizing smell on antique military tanks and turbine blades. Curled scraps of metal littered the muddy ground. One of the most remarkable structures appeared to be an abandoned turquoise train, where a colorful icon of a saint was pictured in each window. As I would later come to know, the train had become a bastion of the Ogedei's polytheistic religion, the glue that motivated and inspired the village's inhabitants to practice virtuous traits of hospitality and peace.

"This is old military base from war," Z told me, pausing on hauling the coal to point out the tall wired electrical fixtures. "We use it to live now."

I noticed the rusty, metal, boxlike structures scattered in an anthropologically thought-out way, while neat hills of metal lay around.

"It looks busy, even in the morning," I said, spinning the coal shovel's handle playfully. "Why was this base built? Physical wars are obsolete."

"It's from the War of 2034," said Z, then motioned with his hands to a circular structure. "This base, it's last physical one from then. But now, no more physical war. Only cyber war."

The war had happened when I was a teenager and, naturally, I did not pay attention to it. In fact, I thought that while there were plenty of preparations for it, the physical fighting had only lasted a day.

"That was a short war."

"According to paper, you right," said Z. "But war went on for longer. I was a cyber spy. I worked two year and I thought, 'Ah, I don't like doing this' and came back here."

"What side were you working for?" I asked, but Z hesitated.

"I don't like talking about it—I don't like it," Z said mysteriously and shut down the conversation. *How intriguing*, I thought to myself. *Seems I like I hit a secret nerve.*

Captain Yank yelled at us the equivalent of "faster," which I only picked up from previous experiences with the language. Z and I trudged the coal into the burner faster while I thought of ways to tease out the secret.

"What did you do?" I asked, dropping some coals off. Seeing that Z ignored my question, I switched focus. "Did you enjoy the work?"

Z paused and dabbed his forehead with an old-fashioned handkerchief.

"No." He bit his lip in frustration. "I helped cause too much chaos that turned into a lot of physical dead people in street."

The barge had come to a full stop while a crowd of the Ogedei's inhabitants gathered around the port as if we were about to hand out Christmas presents. A chorus of gruff dog barks resounded in the distance, and a pregnant, short, stocky woman in a colorful red skirt approached us, menacingly tossing her thick, dark braid behind her. She took one look at me from five yards away and then heatedly yelled at Captain Yank in a foreign language, calling the attention of others. The boat's crew stepped off the barge, a signal to unpack the goods on the ship for the youth. Some of them openly stared at me with friendly curiosity, while others ignored me with stonewall faces.

Captain Yank pulled me by the shoulders to stand beside him while he patiently explained something to the angry pregnant woman. I smiled at her in acknowledgment while she scowled at me; I thought I saw a tinge of fear in her expression. I later learned the pregnant woman was Yorbuta—Captain Yank's equivalent of a wife.

They must be talking about me, I realized. *These people would hardly be allowed to enter NK City. The reverse must be true too.*

I could see the same controversial divide in the younger members of the crowd that were staring at me. I am not one for public speaking, but here I felt as if a vindicating monologue was demanded of me. The same bushy, black eyebrows with broad, flat noses were staring at me with judgment, curiosity, confusion, and apathy. I was like a pig being put out for slaughter for the

entertainment of the crowd.

Eventually the gossiping racket died down, and as quickly as the group had congregated, everyone turned on a heel and left to continue their work. Z, relieved the stressful social confrontation was over, pulled me along to his hut. My-Ra ran in front of us, happy to be off the cramped boat. She would constantly race too far forward, see that we were lagging behind, then circle around us.

Walking through the land of the Ogedei, I finally had a better view of the inhabitants. Some aspects of the village shocked me, such as the children running outside with no accompanying safety Corts. Some aspects were recognizable, like the groups of girls who strayed far from the popular childish games to instead talk to each other while occasionally throwing a bread crumb to a begging seagull.

The children of Ogedei were prematurely introduced to the art of pushing and moving heavy scraps of metal with the use of pulleys and a supreme knowledge of ropes. Another cultural aspect that was shocking for me to learn was that if a child showed a hint of intellectual genius, the young scholar would be introduced to the art of metal smelting at as young as ten years old. Others were sorted into the broad-shouldered youth that would carry carts of wrenches, hammers, and saws. Domestic matters were in the hands of the older population; the parents of the children were busy tending to the cows, milking them or throwing some nasty slop to feed the pigs. The elders also did not rest and, with an air of meditation, they would cast their nets into the shore water. The only relaxed creatures were the stray tortoise cats that languidly lay in hidden spots until a human approached them. Then, they would run away to a new hiding spot in a fluster.

Z's hut was, as I expected, messy and cozy at the same time. The rusty, brown walls were covered in thick wool rugs hanging off nails. One rug displayed colorful geometric shapes with earth tones, and another full-sized rug had a beautiful, hazel-colored lake clearing ringed with birch trees. An old-fashioned handmade topographical map of a forest hung on the other side of the room. The room had more bookshelves than modern libraries do. I fingered through the titles—red, blue, grimy, paperback, falling apart, barely touched.

"This way." Z guided me through a narrow hallway to what looked like a kitchen.

The kitchen mixed dining quarters of the house smelt of garlic, reminiscent of five-star cooking. At the table sat a strange-looking woman, whom Z approached and gave a gentle forehead kiss. Draped around her shoulders was a scarlet shawl, and from underneath I could see hideous metal wires for fingers that she used to set down a spoon. Her fine motor movements were mechanical and lacked the fluidity that normal fingers have. I didn't want to look too hard out of disrespect, but sometimes seeing abnormal humans makes you look harder.

"Hello." She was the first person to greet me with proper language that lacked any accent. "My name is G." She crossed a hand over the table. We politely tapped the palms of our hands—tapping worked because she couldn't quite grasp my hand into a proper handshake. I introduced myself as Z tapped a spare chair to sit me down.

"Are your names typical?" I asked. Z scrunched up his mouth to the side, giving G a side glance.

"Hm," Z hummed, exchanging a look with G and making her laugh.

"No," she explained. "It's a form of identification that we hide away."

"Sure," I said, not understanding. *Is this all to do with Z being a cyber spy?*

"I don't use my real name. I'm Z," Z said mysteriously. "No one can hunt me down anymore. I mean, metal hawks try to catch any person who look like me, but those are easy to destroy."

"You are being hunted down?" I asked. In NK City, people were hunted down for committing serious atrocities like murder. *Was I about to have breakfast with murderers?*

"Don't worry about it," G reassured me. "He's not a murderer. That's all you need to know."

CHAPTER 14

REBORN

After such a terrible experience being seasick in combination with the brunt of digestive issues, I was more than pleased to be able to go on walks outside. Most of the adults in the Ogedei had mixed reactions when they saw me—fear, distrust—but the children of the village and I became acquaintances immediately. Both of us were curious about the other; the children were curious what a "city lady" was like and I was curious what these "outsider kids" were like. Language communication was impaired, but playing classic games like tag or hide and seek are universal to all cultures, even if Ogedei was in the forgotten land of NK. My first few days were consumed by playing monster until my young friends wore out and developed crimson cheeks. Like starving domestic animals, they would run to their huts and happily chomp away at sugar canes they had stolen from their homes to share with me. While the food quality did not compare to NK City, sugar canes and condensed milk were delicacies here that I had become fond of.

I met Captain Yank's youngest child, his seven-year-old daughter Nia, who loved to play the Ogedei equivalent of "house." I picked up phrases in the Ogedei language, like *eh-zh* (meaning mother) and, the most special to Nia, *huhed* (meaning baby). Nia was the most excited about her unborn sibling. She showed me the ragged painted dolls that she and her sister would play with and the hair styles she was planning to braid her sibling's hair. I doubt she knew the sibling's gender, but it was obvious to me that she wanted a sister.

One morning, a week after the barge had docked, someone rapped at the hut's door. Because G lacked the motor skills required to open the door, I opened it up to see no one—until I looked down and saw Nia's doe eyes that were brimming with worry.

"What is it?" I asked her.

She said something excitedly and pulled at my hand. I didn't catch anything that she said except for "eh-zh."

I motioned for an imaginary, round stomach. "Eh-zh?" I asked her. Nia nodded and pulled my hand, screaming something in Ogedei.

The sprint was on to catch the child of a pregnant woman who hated me. A woman's body naturally knows what to do, but childbirth was far from my specialty, although Nia's urgency made me shy to say no.

We rushed past the gaping children on the streets and the flimsy, curved bridges over the streams. Yorbuta was generally displeased that an outsider like me had been escorted to Ogedei. In fact, while the rest of the original crew from the barge had visited me, Captain Yank was the only one who didn't visit me to please his wife.

I didn't need Nia as a guide to indicate which house Yorbuta lived in, because her screams sounded demonic. Over her was the red-nosed Captain Yank, clutching her hand in a nervous shower of sweat. The local healer—tense and sweating too—was prepping medicine, reciting clicks and rolls, and encouraging the mother as she groaned in pain.

The healer looked up with her wet curls covering her eyes and waved me closer to the canal; the child's wrinkly, deformed forehead had emerged. The baby was crowning with the face up, which is not how births are supposed to present. With the proper technology and medicine, Yorbuta would have received a Cesarean birth in NK City because the baby could suffocate and die. I was horrified at how mangled and bruised the baby's face was with violet and pink colors kissing her. My hands shook at the adrenaline of the complicated situation, and I approached Yorbuta's birthing canal on my knees.

The burden of the task was shared by me and the healer. I cupped the child's head, trying to keep the baby's neck in line as waves of contractions rolled over the mother. Yorbuta screamed at me, adjusted her position, then threw her head back once the contraction was done. In normal circumstances, this hateful scream would have been a signal to run away. The healer recited a chant while Captain Yank cried salty tears that mixed with Yorbuta's sweat.

The child's swollen skull was now in my two quivering hands. I could feel the thick head of hair slipping between my middle and ring fingers. I tried to regain a better position. Was the child even alive? I couldn't hear any noise or whimpering from the being.

The mother roared and the right shoulder poked out of the folds. The limb was twisted and irregular.

"Come on, come on!" I encouraged her in English as the mother wept.

Another wave pushed the child's opposite shoulder out. I stooped over to become a bigger base of support because the child was about to be fully born and it was already slippery with fluid. The next moment, the entire baby was out, and I nearly dropped it like an idiot.

There I stood, in the middle of a decrepit military bunker, with a purple, wrinkled baby whom I hadn't a clue how to hold or take care of properly. The child was still connected to its mother's cord while Captain Yank was still grasping his wife's pale knuckles.

With the healer's help, we tucked the baby into a swaddle. I must have been holding the baby wrong, because she took the child away with a concerned look. The healer had taken a sack and started sucking out the liquid from the child's mouth.

I rubbed the baby's slippery chest, praying for a sound.

The baby let out the tiniest of unhappy yelps. A collective sigh of relief was released, and someone squealed in the corner. The healer rubbed the bloody, purple child even more aggressively. Babies don't come out perfect, but they can't stay purple.

Yorbuta asked something about the baby, and I nodded back to emotionally calm her. The healer was focused on the baby but mumbled an answer to Yorbuta's question.

After many yelps and squeals from the child, she became a less disturbing skin tone. Quivering with the high of holding an absolute alien, I passed on the tiny bundle of delicate to feed on her mother.

"Chanti!" The healer screamed a heavenly name for the newborn. "Chanti!"

~

As G explained, it was customary to celebrate a child's birth with a local parade to the train temple. Yorbuta was helped into a bright yellow covering with easy access to her breast for feeding and was pushed along in a chair. Captain Yank's beard had been carefully trimmed with a meticulous hand, and the rest of the children followed behind, each bundled into a silver brocade.

Cymbals and celebratory mobile xylophones followed Captain Yank, Yorbuta, Baine, Jerimiem, Nia, and their newborn Chanti. I was pulled along the crowd too into the lengthy, turquoise abandoned train that stood off of the tracks. I was ushered into a rectangular hallway that was dotted with candles and bronze statues, and the walls were painted with primal murals of crimson, amber, and forest green. It smelt of smoldering incense and derelict junkyard. Although an odd combination, I liked it.

The ruin was strange, but it felt in theme with the rest of Ogedei. There was thickened red candle wax, a freshly grazed pine wood floor, delicately polished statues, and a rich velvet carpet to tread on. I saw sun-crisped faces who eagerly approached me, touched my hands with their warm, roughened hands, and shook mine with gratitude.

The healer led the way, clicking and chanting. She was asking for goodness and cleverness for Chanti and for good luck and safety for Yorbuta.

I was still in shock from the delivery that occurred only two hours earlier. Despite her previous disdain for me, Yorbuta asked me to do the honor of pinning a metallic rose pin onto her baby's wrap. The healer then cradled the child in her arms and began singing. A chorus of people joined in, clashing with the baby's unhappy wail like a moving tide of emotions, scratching the surface of an old memory.

I don't like ceremonies. My mother's funeral was hardly a celebration of her life and felt like a catfight over money. But without even speaking to the group of train gatherers, I felt the sacred joy that had been elusive to me.

After Chanti's birth, the stigma surrounding me began to dissipate. I continued slowly learning the language of the settlement and used it when greeting people who came to visit me. I became known within the village as the "Flying Healer." I had protested the title, but there was no distinction here between the languages—a healer is still a healer. People kept filtering into the hut with complaints that I had no tools to solve. I would hear them say, "My stomach hurts," or "my leg hurts," but none suffered from anything as serious as a heart attack. Other than recommending taking a break from hauling metallic junk, I couldn't recommend much more, and it frustrated me.

Another cultural point about the settlement that I found fascinating was that these people depended heavily on each other's roles for survival; this made everyone work hard to maintain a high level of productivity. There were the maritime matters, the livestock to be taken care of, the children to babysit and raise, and the mechanics. One would think that G couldn't contribute because of her disabilities, but her background in chemistry was useful for recycling material, especially when new loads of junk came on the barge.

"How come you have the best language out of everyone here in Ogedei?" I asked her one day over dinner.

"I grew up in *New Jochi*," she told me, stiffly sticking pieces of meat onto her fork.

"And how did you end up here?" I asked. G sighed and stared at Z with romantic tenderness, preparing for a long story.

"Z and I met at a hospital in New Khan." She started her story, then covered her mouth to finish chewing. "I frequented them often. Z was a computer technician and we instantly fell in love. But the same night I confessed my love to him, he told me he was running away from NK City and told me all this nonsense that he was in trouble and had to leave that night. I thought it was so romantic. I went all the way through and ran away with a wanted criminal to this village that Z had grown up in."

"What trouble?" I probed. *Will the secret finally be let out?* G cocked her head, as if asking Z how much he would let me know.

"I told Ary a little," Z explained to her, laid down his fork, and turned to me. "Long time ago, I built base for quantum computer when I was in NK. City people didn't like that. Then, G and I were kicked out once they found out, and I was branded as criminal." He raised his shirt to reveal a hairy chest and briefly flashed a tattoo stamp of a string of digits.

"A what computer?" I asked him, dumbfounded. This was where the boundary of my education lay.

"It's a quantum computer," Z stuttered, his excitement pushing his darkened glasses off the bridge of his nose. "It's one hundred times better than any computer ever. It make calculation quick—" he snapped his fingers "—because of subatomic particle properties that exist in one or two states. Using electron spin and photo polarization, we can model high and low voltage systems, which is how traditional computers encode binary."

That was the most that I had ever heard Z speak. I was in awe because, while I had thought of Z as a practical man, he knew significantly more than I did about the computers that I used to use every day in New Khan.

He stopped to take a deep breath, then continued. "Sub-atomic particles can be used much quick than hanging voltage and, in end, we produce crazy computer! It can solve problems normal computer dream of doing. It is super intelligence."

"Wow," I said, filling in the silence by chewing on poorly seasoned meat. I had respected Z's intelligence, but he was clearly smarter than I had taken him. "Why are you now a criminal for building such a thing?" I asked.

"I don't know. It's a crazy tool. They don't like people knowing. They can control what you buy, what you think, what you eat," Z explained. "Everything will be a bad formula. There'll be an algorithm for—"

"For commercials," G helped him out, tapping an acrylic fingernail into a rhythm. "It'll be manipulative!"

Now that was a conspiracy theory that the older generations of New Khan liked to complain about.

"If the commercials know what you want better than yourself, why not trust that?" I defended, heat rising in my cheeks.

"No, no, listen, that's different." Z waved his hand, then emphasized his next statement with a pointer finger. "You see something and might think, 'Hmph, I don't want to buy!'" Z pouted and folded his arms. "That's ok, algorithm think different. Shows you something else. You think, 'Hm, interesting,' but then forget that you ever wanted something. But then, you see it in real life on your best friend. You think, 'My god! I wanted this for so, so long!' So, you buy—"

"It's a cycle of not having, desiring, and consuming, you know?" G jumped in. "And you restart, feel bad about yourself. You are locked into this illusion of free will."

"And our choices aren't made by us. Here we are free." Z concluded for G, and the two of them nodded at each other in approval. "Ogedei is hardly a place that city recognize anymore, it's so far away. Here I am safe and can do anything.

No one is watching, no one is trying to sell me anything. Only issue is that it's a harder life."

Watching how the two moved as a team, completing and improving upon each other's thoughts, was spectacular. But I could also sense that I was in the minority for this argument.

"My advertisement recommendations are always spot on," I said. "They're helpful for me and I can discover something I would never have known otherwise. I still retain my free will to dislike a song, for example. And then I will never play it again."

"I come from your world, and it wasn't for me," G noted. "I create a lot of my own music, which is now rare. But because I grew up in your world, I am unfortunately programmed to hate some sounds. Like the ones that you listen to and you just want to turn the sound off. I force myself to try to take what I consider terrible sounds and make them even better than the songs that the radio machines create."

"Radio machines?" I asked, laughing awkwardly. "That is a conspiracy."

G shook her head adamantly. "Radio machines make music based on algorithms. The idea is, 'Why have a human torture themselves into agony over chords?' No music is produced by a real person, it's by a program that knows all music theory and knows what will trigger a dopamine release in a human's brain."

"No way," I said. "My favorite musical artist Randy has interviews about her inspirations, how her music changes. I believe it, she's very knowledgeable in what she does."

"It's still a farce," G said. "Do you know how many people and machines are behind one artist? There's the radio machine to make the music, there's the choreographer, there are the managers, the social media marketers, the plastic surgeons, and the stimulating drugs for constant energy. Once she burns out—which she will—there will be no more Randy. She's just a pretty face for music."

My cheeks were heated, as if someone had slapped them over and over. Z clicked in his odd little language to stop arguing with the guest. G conceded and smiled at me with her disgusting yellow teeth. "I'm sorry. When we finish eating, I can show you some of my music if you'd like."

I thought being a nurse taught me to be as nonjudgmental as possible, but living with Z and G revealed them to be the weirdest couple I had ever met. G was born with a condition that left her with nubs for hands, which she explained had been the effect of her mother consuming chemicals while pregnant. As a reclusive man, Z had taken up a hobby of trying to perfect G's prosthetic limbs (I suspected her limbs were a replacement for his original love, the quantum computer). He would dissect old calculators, engines, and electrical wiring in hopes of improving G's limbs. Their hut was a constant collaboration of man, metal, skin, and nails. At one point, I was even included in the project once I revealed that I had some anatomical knowledge. G exhibited her fine motor skills, including her adaptation of playing the guitar. She struggled playing guitar the traditional way. Instead, she would lay the guitar down on her lap and strummed it like a dulcimer.

I learned to enjoy G's music. She knew what tunes I would like and performed them for me, but then she would adopt a mischievous look and play something dissonant. G was like a songbird because she was a fantastic singer, but she also had a keen eye for musical records, yellowing music books, or modular parts for building a new synthesizer. Her decaying body had been one long project that supported her yearning to build new keyboards or construct another unique sound. Together with Z, they would animatedly gush over the capacitors, amplifiers, and inductors they would find when sorting through the metallic junk the barge brought in.

With each week of living in Ogedei, I changed more: I let the children style my hair into their traditional, complex braids and wore a bright-colored yellow skirt with geometric patterns not to fit in, but because I enjoyed feeling the design. I was becoming proficient at the language, my arm stopped swelling and hardly anything bothered me at all after all the near-death experiences. I knew that eventually I would be snuck back into NK City on the next shipment of the barge and, even if I enjoyed Ogedei life, the old thoughts of revenge itched the back of my mind. I still wondered about Lucas, whether unconsciously through dreams or discussing my worries with G. I still had no idea what the chances were that he was alive.

CHAPTER 15

IN THE TRENCHES

———

*"Charlie Bonzabo to Alpha, we are preparing for landing,"
Mom's lips beat against the headphones.*

"Charlie, you are clear. Have a good day."

Mother muttered back a reply.

*I felt the familiar jolt of the plane. I was drowning in a
river I couldn't control. It's the terror of reliving that same déjà
vu. I wanted it to stop, but my hands were gripped to the seat.*

*"Come on, Ary. I want to go home." Mother's delicate eye-
liner lines smudged and a scarlet mark from broken glass
kissed her face. Especially once her dementia became severe,
she begged me to leave in this way. She had fallen and was
dangling upside down, with the glass enveloping us in a cloud
of danger. Her voice changed deeper, gruffer, into a grunt akin
to Lucas's.*

*"Why won't you save me?" She cried with Lucas's mus-
tache visible.*

The S-440 nightmare liked to replay itself like a broken
record. I like to think of it as the brain wanting to slow
down that finite amount of time before something terrible
jolted the brain. I remember it all, from the sacrilege of our
perfectly packed S-440 to the smell of burning fumes that
could swallow us whole. The platitude of every day allowed

my S-440 nightmares to morph into wondering about my late crewmates.

Several weeks had passed since I first docked at the Ogedei port, and my time was coming to an end. That same morning, the barge was to be reloaded again with old metal supplies to sell on the black markets near NK City. The timeline for reloading would take five days of heavy lifting, inventory, and reorganizing. Being part of the crew to board, I was to play an active role in helping with the grunt work of carrying the next shipment of metal scraps to the barge. To fuel up for the exercise, I ate a peaceful breakfast of hardly aged cheese and milk while G played a musical accompaniment with her makeshift guitar hand. Once I was finished with my meal, I helped tend to G's handmade prosthetics (this was mainly cleaning the gunk and re-oiling under Z's guidance) while G asked me how I slept. This is a regular question that I always gave harmless answers to, but her question reminded me of the fresh set of nightmares.

"I dreamt a lot about my crewmates," I answered earnestly. "The dream morphs often but now it's my dead crewmates asking for help."

"Good thing you know death scare you," Z said, loosening a bolt on G's elbow. "Appreciate those emotion."

"I don't want to be reminded of the crash," I protested. "I want to forget about it."

"What he means is that you should be able to feel sad," G corrected, flexing her shiny forearm. "Distraction will only bring you back to the shock."

"I feel at fault for my crewmates dying," I said. "I could have poisoned myself. I was close to eating the same poison."

"One is certainly dead," G said. "But what are the chances the other is dead?"

Z laughed, using pliers to tighten a clamp standing in for a pronator muscle. "Captain Eli came back from a similar barge trip. He might know something about your Luca."

"Really?" I asked, feeling a glimmer of hope. "What are the chances that you could arrange a meeting?"

~

I met Captain Eli in the presence of my hosts over a languid breakfast of pipe tobacco, condensed milk with coffee, and cheese sandwiches. Truthfully, he was a rather handsome young man in his thirties. While he still had the typical bushy black eyebrows and skin darkened by the sun, his complexion was well balanced. He had a chiseled jaw and a neatly trimmed beard. Never mind his looks, because the story he told of Lucas was even more interesting.

"My crew and I had no intention of searching the forest," he began telling me through G's translation. "My apprentice noticed that something was falling out of the sky while smoking that was not a metal hawk. It looked like it could be a valuable treasure with parts that would sell well in the market. We figured that it would have fallen close to a riverbank."

"Was this river bank a rocky one without much sand?" I asked.

"Yes, that part tends to be rocky with a lot of rushing water," he confirmed. I leaned in because I was still unsure about some of the vocabulary and looked to G for translation. "But we couldn't leave the barge in shallow water. Half of us split up to row closer to the shallow parts. It was dangerous," Captain Eli admitted. "And at first, it didn't seem promising at all. We searched for two days until we finally came upon a helicopter."

"A helicopter!" G exclaimed the translation. I grabbed a piece of paper to write out the square title belonging to the home I knew so well: S-440.

"Was this written on it?" I asked him, showing him the sketch. He nodded.

"Yes. Beside it, we found an old man who was combative with us. He had white gray hair and a mustache and a crooked back." The captain went on with his story. "No one spoke his language and he did not want to cooperate with us."

"That sounds like Lucas," I trembled. "What did you do with him?"

"Believe me, we really did try to help him," he said. "When we offered him food, he ate it like a savage. We took the technology that we could carry on our small row boats and tried to push him onto our boats. He was so stubborn and adamant, but we couldn't understand why. He looked like he was starving! I should have let him go, but my apprentice sedated him. My apprentice is smart in some ways, but also an impulsive fool, I'm sorry." Captain Eli bowed his head in apology.

"He didn't want to leave without me," I whispered, clutching my hands to my chest. "Then what happened?"

"He traveled with us for a while, unhappily. We treated him well, but we hardly spoke his language. He must've thought he could get back to NK City on his own. The morning after we finished our hike back to the barge, we found that he had run off in the middle of the night with a lot of our supplies," Captain Eli said. "I would say that he has a chance of dying in the wild, but he seemed like a sturdy man. There's a bigger chance that he was captured by the metal hawks by now."

"I have to save him," I said, determined. *Lucas did not want to leave me alone despite our disagreements. He was trying to delay until I came back.*

"We are still leaving port in five days." Z told me. But the story was starting to make sense in my head.

"I left that day for a long time. I was trying to hunt and it seems that Captain Eli's barge attempted to rescue him while I was gone." I pieced the story together. "Lucas may seem aggressive to the Ogedei, but knowing him, he was probably shouting about staying behind. He didn't leave me on purpose. Although," I turned to look sternly at Captain Eli, "why would anyone sedate that man?"

An awkward hush fell over the hut. Captain Eli bowed his head.

"It was miscommunication coming from me and should have never happened," he said. "I'm sorry. At first, we were only going to take the items from the helicopter and leave him once he had been accidentally sedated. But we were afraid of the gods being angry with us and turned back to bring him with us."

"My goodness." G clutched a metal fist to her chest. "You really played into the stereotype of savages."

"Do you think he's dead?" I asked him coldly.

Captain Eli hesitated.

"No. I expect he's in the captivity of the metal hawks now," he said.

"If Lucas is still alive in the custody of the metal hawks, I think we should save him," I said. G nodded her head in agreement.

"Hunting metal hawk take lots training," Z butted into the conversation.

"I would like to learn how to hunt them," I insisted. "If there's a chance that he is alive, I want to find him."

"You can't hunt them alone."

"I don't plan to. I think that there's a good reason that my mom appears in my dreams. She's telling me something and if there's a chance that he's alive, I'd like to take it."

"Who relies on dreams to talk to dead men?" Z mocked.

"He's not dead!"

"Every bipedal human in metal hawk robot eyes is me. You may be Ary, but to them you are criminal of NK City," Z said.

After adjusting G's hand into an anatomically correct position, he stuck his pipe in between his thin discolored lips. I sat back with my arms crossed, visibly upset. G poked into his arm to silently encourage Z.

"Ok." He sighed with exasperation. "This a tricky situation and we look bad. NK City does not know about Ogedei and has no rule over us. But I do not want to give NK City any small reason to find and bomb us." He turned to me. "If he was truly captured, there's only one place that he'd be. In the metal hawk nest. I can train you in my free time and we will see if he's in the nest on the way to the city."

I thanked him for his mentorship, which seemed to appease the deepened lines of stress on his face. Training began that same day with a background on the metal hawks.

"This training is basic," Z motioned with his hands to show the level. "You can't do much. You are only going to learn crossbow skills and then practice rock climbing. Once we actually get there, listen to me if you want survive."

Metal hawks relied on facial and body recognition of humans, which meant that if anything resembled a bipedal human they would be taken in as suspects. The sheer number of hawks at their nest was dangerous, and they would easily overtake even a skilled hunter on their own. They patrolled their nest and never ate, slept, or thought hard if anything resembled a human. One or two metal hawks would not be too difficult to beat as I knew from personal experience, but a whole party of metal hawks would disarm a human until the human either starved to death or was sent for "sorting."

My baseline skill for crossbow shooting was below mediocre at best. Z was becoming noticeably frazzled and, to save himself the bother, he referred me to Baine for extra instruction. At first, I was happy to have a female mentor teaching me until Baine snapped at me for not hitting any bull's-eye targets. I was surprised by the drastic change in our relationship because Baine had been my first friend and now showed her impatient teaching side. Two months ago, I would have been hyperfocused on the criticism she gave me. But now I was focused on perfecting my aim and contributing anything to rescue Lucas.

My poorly constructed crossbow also had a knack for falling apart randomly. Z was shocked when I told him I didn't know what a screwdriver was, and he was forced to teach me how to use toolbox materials that would be attached to a waist belt consisting of a screwdriver, a hammer, and a miscellaneous chisel.

Rope climbing was significantly more relaxed and under the instruction of Jerimiem. After a brief review of important knots, most of the time was spent joking and racing up to the top of the practice boulder where the anchor was. Even though my upper-arm strength was terrible, Jerimiem was a supportive belayer.

"Of course, we never want to be climbing and fighting at the same time," he'd tell me. "It rarely happens nowadays because we at first disorient them with distraction grenades and then attack."

Each day, I would repeat my skills again in front of Z and was met with disappointment from him. He was a hard-to-please mentor and gave out criticism with the same freedom that the little Ogedei girls would throw breadcrumbs for the birds. "If you make a silly mistake like that, you will get us killed," he told me with a grim face after I forgot to properly secure a rope. After I was dismissed, I felt horrid about my performance. *I needed to hear that criticism*, I thought to myself in an effort to preserve my ego. *I don't want to die while attempting to rescue Lucas.*

As the days counted down, what started as hope to find Lucas and to learn a new set of skills waned into frustration over my sore muscles. On the outside, I tried to show that I was putting in maximal effort and that I was confident, but the reality was that I felt the gravity of my incompetence.

CHAPTER 16

FLYING AGAIN

The barge's capacity visually represented when my time at the settlement would be over. By the fifth day, the deck of the rusty boat was lined with neat rows of smelted aluminum, iron, and copper. There were refurbished motherboards, multicolored cords and wires, transistors, and blackened matte screens from TVs. To me, the barge felt like a pleasing museum display where I could find the video game console I had dreamed of as a child lying in what was considered a worthless pile. This console was a fulfillment of dreams and a scrapbook filled with memories of feeling accomplishment and pleasure.

On day four, Z laid out his plan for investigating the metal hawk nest for the chance that Lucas was captured by them. The metal hawk nest, according to Baine's sketch, was an upside-down cone with an entrance and exit at the peak of the nest. The metal hawks would capture anyone who looked remotely human to be sent for "sorting" in the real world into two terrible options happening afterward: If a captured person matched a criminal known in NK City, they would be put on trial with a high chance of the death penalty because of their escape from New Khan. If a captured person didn't match a criminal description, they would still be put on a sentence for possible "intent to escape."

First, antique radar detectors would be used to approximate where the nest of the metal hawks was. Once the nest was found, the plan was to hike until the hawks signaled each other to begin the attack.

Once the attack began, phase two of the plan was to disorient the birds with magnetic pellets. This was a recent invention designed by Z to disturb metal hawks' sense of direction and spatial navigation, effectively blinding them for an attack. The metal hawk programming changed often, as did the compass pellets, but Z seemed confident that with his experience, he could take them down without assistance. Once the metal hawks were disoriented, it was Baine's job to destroy them using a special heavy crossbow and for the rest of us to act as support.

The plan reignited that reunification with Lucas was a concrete possibility, not just a nightmare. Now with this multitiered plan rehearsed, the crew dismissed itself to a nightly feast prior to our departure. I helped slowly chop the firewood while minding my sore muscles and deep in thoughts of Lucas's rescue.

As I waited for the feast to start, I snuck away to practice using a crossbow one more time. Although Baine's instruction was harsh, I appreciated the amount of time she put into training me. Over the course of four days, my bull's-eye target success ratio rate improved from one-twentieth of the time to one-seventh of the time. Anything that could help against the metal hawks and rescuing Lucas was a success.

The feast tables looked stunning enough to take my mind off the rescue. They were clad with colorful bowls of pork, plates of pickled veggies, cheeses cut into thumb-sized parts, and fizzling fermented drinks. With G's translating assistance, people exchanged their stories about previous hunts on the metal hawks. Some people had positive stories about personal growth and lauded Z for his leadership.

One story that stuck with me was the disappearance of a mother's child who was never found in the nest. Despite the language barrier, I could sense the mother was earnestly hoping to convince me to drop the expedition. "They're not hard to hunt," I could understand her simple language. "But if something goes wrong, they will not hesitate."

I said goodbye to baby Chanti, whom I had seen emerge only a week ago, with a forehead kiss. Yorbuta graced me with a delicate green scarf with recycled pieces of gold sewn in. I had grown rooted and attached to my small cot, the thick rugs covering the walls, and the pine dust that accented the unique situation I was in. I had hated the dust, antique lamps, and the general clutter present, but now I felt attached.

The most difficult goodbye was with G on the morning of the barge's departure; our relationship had become comfortable and one of caring for the other. G tended to my needs like a mother while I maintained upkeep of her handmade prosthetics. She entertained me with her experimental music while I entertained her with stories on how NK City had changed over the years. Talking to her made me miss my home.

"I will visit," I reassured her. "I'll tie up my loose ends, present my case, and then I'll be back once again."

G cocked her head to one side.

"We do ask that you don't try to find us again," she said.

"Why?" I asked, feeling a panic in the unfolding plans.

"We are free here but that comes at the cost of being hardly protected. Taking you back in puts the discovery of our cluster in danger," G told me.

"You don't trust me?" I asked, offended.

"Like you, I came from New Khan. And of course, I found family in Z and My-Ra and living off metal. I have no desire to go back. And if I did, I know that I would never be able to live the same life again."

"You think I would tell on you? Or come back to be a spy?"

"You were in such a pathetic state when we found you that we figured that you weren't a spy," G laughed.

I felt offended at first, but then I remembered my own scrappy reflection in the mirror. She pulled me with cold, hard hands into a hug.

"It was nice to know you," said G. I could feel her chest vibrate as she spoke.

"We really won't see each other again?" I asked. "Is this your way of saying that we will never speak again?"

She pulled away and smiled. "It'll be okay, all is well."

Her ambivalent words stung with rejection.

The barge undocked once the morning dawn had blazed its watercolor shades, while the early seabirds flew around to beg for a crumb. When I first arrived, I was greeted with hostility and apprehension, but the crowd at the dock waved back a goodbye.

The journey on the barge began uneventfully as Z had narrowed down the location of the nest and we followed the southern wind for several days. By now, our roles on the boat and as hunters were well defined. I was the barge's cleaner and also assigned to check inventory of the supplies every single day. On top of these duties, Baine would wear me out with more crossbow training. Jerimiem sympathized with me and joked that Baine and I were playing a game of hide and seek. I was willing to practice, but I preferred the method without social embarrassment. "You're thinking too hard," she'd snap at me, and I remembered this criticism. "The way you're shooting couldn't kill a sloth."

After sailing for two days, Captain Yank and Z concluded to dock the barge and for the crew to begin packing. There was too much gear and junk to move around: the crossbows, arrows, tools, harnesses, and climbing gear made for a heavy load. Captain Yank recited a small prayer under his breath on the beachy shore and the trek with our bulk began.

I was anxious to see the nest. Fighting two metal hawks was exhausting but not impossible; fighting dozens of metal hawks sounded challenging and overwhelming.

The nest was not located far from the barge, and it was obvious we were in metal hawk territory. They swarmed above us in the open sky as we crouched through shrubbery in a chance to avoid them and bide our time. I was surprised we even had a chance to see the nest unseen, but not for long.

The nest looked similar to the image Baine had sketched for me— a beehive-like structure with intricately woven barbed wire that created a roof with a steep slope. About twelve proud bastards clung on to the wires, crowding around the rooftop that contained both the entrance and exit of the den at the top of the mound. Their red laser eyes were pointed in all cardinal directions. I shivered looking at the metal hawks. We all crouched down in our camouflage-colored clothing to get a better view and prepare for a battle.

Z signaled to us silently and released his distraction grenade, immediately catching the metal hawks' eyes. In a split second, the metal hawks shrieked a terrible sound to alert a swarm of metal hawks that emerged from their nest. It seemed as if they flew ten times faster the moment they saw Z, excited to fulfill their programming duty. Their shrieking alarms were terrifying. One by one, the biggest leading the pact, the metal hawks rose into the air away from the nest into a defensive position. Z fired off the first distraction grenade and it worked like magic. All of the metal hawks in midair quivered and short circuited, falling onto the ground like dead insects.

"That was easy," I said, cringing at the sight of the metallic beasts on the ground. Z shook his head at me.

"No, that was too easy," he said. "Cover your ears again."

He fired off another distraction grenade for safe measure as Baine shot at the wings of the metal hawks to permanently disable them. The scene was eerily still, and even I felt uncomfortable that such beasts were easily tamed. Nevertheless, Jerimiem motioned to move forward with the plan to put on our harnesses for the climb up to the top of the nest.

Shering led the climb while I slowly brought up the rear, my elbow pain coming back sharper than ever. I looked up and almost everyone was near the top, while I had barely hit the midway point. No sooner had Z reached the top than the bellow of the metallic hawks cut the euphoria short.

There was hideous screeching and shaking in the nest from underneath of me. I looked up to see a dark cloud of metallic hawks rising out of the pit at the top. Even the seemingly dead metallic hawks had feigned weakness and were rising upon us. The volume of wings and beaks and angry laser eyes was overwhelming. We were all stunned. The arrows had to fly.

The original plan was unfolding faster than a fire swallowing paper. There was no clear leadership in the moment, just the panicked example of the rest of the crew drawing back their arrows to shoot. Fighting off the metal hawks was supposed to have been completed separately from climbing up the nest to the opening. Here we were, dangling off of our climbing ropes and swinging from the gravity of shooting off arrows. I had to do my part and support the fight against the metal hawks.

One wing down. The metal hawk screeched.

Jerimiem led the way up the rope to the top of the nest, stopping every couple of paces and shooting an arrow to an upcoming bird. Z followed behind him, climbing and shooting arrows like a hero. I had fallen far behind in the climbing, instead taking advantage of the metal hawks' buffering to shoot out more arrows.

I shot one bird, then another. It felt like a crazy video game! I was bursting with adrenaline. I looked up the nest to see if Z could see how well I was doing. But Z was shaking from difficulty balancing. His boots lost their grip on the slippery metal. And in the next moment, he was sliding down the nest past me. Multiple birds, excited for their trained prey, leaped after him.

"Z!" I yelled.

Attached to nothing, I leaped after him.

I slipped and fell on the roof of the nest because of my ineptitude. In the adrenaline rush of plans changing, I forgot to secure my harness properly, the same mistake I had displayed when training.

I was falling faster than the S-440. In slow motion, I saw a few lone metal hawks shrieking with glee as they saw me as one fewer pesky human to deal with. Z disappeared behind a cloud of fluttering wings, and I was heading straight for the pack.

I tried to dig my heels into the wires. I was scratched up and quickly losing control. I slipped closer to the pack of metal hawks, bleeding and scratching my hands. I was screaming without even recognizing. Z was picked up by a metallic hawk that slammed him into the nest's roof. It looked at least painful and at worst deadly.

I went tumbling into the pseudo pack, which quickly disbanded in order to reach its new target—me. I was still sliding down the nest's roof while they watched me carnivorously in midflight.

At last, I stopped slipping. It seemed that my shirt had caused enough friction for a golden moment. Adrenaline shook my hands, but my vision through the crossbow's kisser was as clear as day. I pulled out the heavy crossbow to set the arrows into the point. Fire one, fire two. *I am an automaton.* I had fired away at the metal hawks closest to me, then crawled up the roof to have a better view of the metal hawk beating up Z. In two tries, I successfully fired for the metal hawk to loosen its grip on Z. I didn't know what happened next, because at least four metal hawks had sprung behind me.

Fire, fire!

A smaller metal hawk swayed away, clutching his injured wing close to his body. Another fell like a dead brown leaf. A chorus of shrieks rose, and multiple red lasers blinded me.

I fired away into the red neon beam of eyes without a care. *This might be a last huzzah.*

Something hit me in the face—a rope from above. It was safety, a more stable position to fight from. *Shoot blindly. Go for the rope.*

I reached for the rope and secured myself, but a second too late I realized that my shoulder was being gripped tightly by a familiar metal talon. I wasn't standing anymore; I was being picked up and pulled away from the rope. I was being swayed to and fro like the balls in Newton's cradle. I was about to be thrown hard against the metal nest just like they had done to Z.

With my nondominant hand, I reached for a chisel in my pocket and stuck it upward into the joints of the bird's metatarsus. It shrieked and loosened its grip on my shoulder. *Clearly it worked*. Next, I slammed a hammer into the metallic talon on my shoulder. In the next moment, I tumbled down back onto the roof of the nest. The rope was closer, but I didn't want to double task anymore and held my ground, shooting any creature that came close.

The laser eyes of the flock stopped blinding as much because of the collective destruction of the birds. The last of the metal hawks fell. Hesitantly, I peeked over the height of the nest to see a pile of them laying upside down on the grass like dead insects.

Z hiked down from his elevated point to help me up. His face was bloodied, he was bleeding out of his mouth, but he was okay.

"Are you alright?" I asked him.

"That was a performance." He ignored my question, pulling me back up to a stand. For someone who is professional and always critical, that was the most positively neutral comment he had ever made to me.

Our hunting crew split into two groups. Z and Shering would stay back to harvest the valuable parts of the metal hawks while the rest would finish hiking to the top of the nest cap where the entrance was. After a brief pipe smoking session, the crew split into halves.

The inside of the nest was hardly visible from outside of the hole. I was demoted to holding a light from above and maintaining the Prusik knots and the rigged ropes while Jerimiem and Baine descended into the inside of the nest.

Once again, time warped into its strange ebb and flow. One hour passed where I sat with my legs on the edge of the entrance to pick at my scabs. Another passed where, instead of sitting, I rolled onto my stomach, worrying myself into tears whether Lucas was alive. Then I would become uncomfortable and readjust into another uncomfortable position.

Jerimiem called out something to me that sounded like gurgling.

"I can't hear!" I called back, my voice distorting in the echo.

"Want good news or bad news?" he called down from below.

"Both!" I yelled back.

"I found him. He look dead!"

CHAPTER 17

ON UNSTEADY LEGS AGAIN

———

Lucas's mangled body was horrifying to look at. Across his gray-haired arms, he had been branded with numbers. He had a nasty bruise on his brow line, and his eyes were black, as if the metal hawks had slammed him against any hard surface possible.

"Oh no," I said as I helped Jerimiem heave him out of the nest. He looked terrible.

"If he's dead, we should leave him," said Baine. "Time is ticking." I scowled and felt for a pulse. He had a slow, weak pulse.

He was breathing normally, which is unexpected for a significantly stressed body. I tried to wake him up with painful stimuli and he responded groggily. *If only I had the right resources to help him*, I thought.

"He looks alive," I said confidently. "He does need a lot of care."

"Everything is down by the barge, so we have to move along. The new metal hawks are being dispatched right now to smear us into pieces, and we have to haul this man down. It's a time bomb."

With great difficulty, we attached his deadweight body to a pulley system along with a partner to pull him down to safety. We took turns hauling Lucas on our shoulders. He would occasionally wake up and grunt, but not much would happen.

The journey back to the barge was more than stressful. The hawks weighed heavily on our minds, and any movement in the sky caused terror within us until we confirmed that it wasn't them. The ground was uneven and tree roots tripped me. I was hungry, tired, and generally concerned about Lucas's condition. I had failed Lorraine, but I was determined to not fail Lucas.

The last valuables of the metal hawks were harvested and added to the collection aboard the deck. Lucas was heaved onto the deck and the crew crowded around. Captain Yank pulled out a small glass bottle and stuck the opening beneath Lucas's nostril. Lucas woke up with a start and blinked hard.

"Get him some food and water," I commanded. Jerimiem gave me his canteen. I pried Lucas's bloodied mouth open and splashed water all over.

This time, I needed to take even better care of him than I had taken of Lorraine. I didn't want to be the last person from the S-440 to face Paul in court.

The barge set sail following the icy, southwest wind. In my delirious mind, I hoped staying awake day and night would be the reason Lucas lived, so I resisted sleep. Regardless, I slept the first barge night like a dead man, rocked by the roar of the engine.

With the help of the sniffing liquid, Lucas's condition improved. He started waking up on his own and drinking fresh water. Previously, I would pour water into his mouth, hoping he wouldn't choke. His face had been battered to the point that reading any type of expression was next to impossible, but he was in obvious pain.

On the third day, Lucas was finally awake enough to conversate. I used to be annoyed at how talkative he was, but this was the first time that I appreciated his story.

"After our argument, I fell asleep outside when these wild barbarians came in. They started grabbin' me and pullin' me."

"I met who you're talking about," I jumped in. Lucas cocked his head.

"Really?"

"They're not barbarians, they're just a bit different from us," I told him. "They told me they were trying to rescue you without sharing a common language with you."

"They looked barbaric anyway. I was trying to tell them to wait—I wanted for you to join in—and they knocked me the hell out. I was mighty pissed!"

"As you should. I was upset when I heard about that," I jumped in.

"Yeah, quit interruptin' me. Anyway, I was plottin' how I'd leave and one night I took everything I could from the barbarians to survive, and I ran. Those people are mighty fools, too, willing to trust a stranger they found in a ruin. I did real well on my own. I was doing quite well. I set up my own home, set up traps, until one of those damn birds attacked me. Well, they're scary as shit, but they aren't that difficult to fight off. I fought 'em off and then the next day, an even bigger swarm came. There were so many of them! They threw me into that hole to rot."

"Sounds like you had a good time while it lasted," I said. Lucas showed me his purple hands.

"Yeah, these boys hurt me so much I cried again. I was thinkin' bout you and Lo and wished for them pain meds. That's the only way to live out here," he said.

"I didn't know if you got kidnapped. I didn't even know whether you were alive!"

"Yeah, I still don't know if I'm alive," Lucas said. "Pinch my shoulder, is this real?"

I pinched him and laughed. "Now, I don't know how you'll take this news, but the boat we are on is from the same 'barbarians.'" Lucas leaned in with a horrified face.

"Are you sure we are going home? Are you sure we aren't going to be roasted on a stick by the end of tonight?" he whispered. "I ain't trust them."

"I know where you're coming from with your history with them, but they would have killed me a long time ago if they had malicious thoughts against me," I told him. *I could have been killed when the metal hawk captured me. I could have been poisoned on the barge. I could have been killed when coming to the village.*

"Tsk, tsk, aren't you naive to be trustin' barbarians and criminals?" Lucas rested his head back onto his pillow. "Are you kidding me?" He laughed nervously, then rose up again. "You speak their language?"

"It's not too difficult to pick up," I said. "I'll teach you some phrases to introduce yourself. It would not be a bad idea to thank them for saving the both of us."

Lucas changed his tone to be softer, as if he didn't want anyone to hear.

"I want to thank you for saving me," he said quietly, then switched back to his pompous, loud tone. "This was a nightmare of a journey. And I ain't piloting again. I hate flying and I hate heights now. Once we sue that bastard, I'm retiring for good."

"I'm happy that you're alive. If I had to bet my money on who'd be most likely to survive, I'd have put my money on you," I told him. Lucas smiled proudly.

"Anyway, how did a skinny chick like you survive without me?"

~

The journey to any destination always seems long-winded and dreary. You pass by landmarks and wonder, "When will I reach the final destination?" But when you are returning from a trip, you know what to expect, and before you know, the journey is over.

As Lucas's condition improved, we talked about what to expect once docking in New Khan. According to Lucas, Lorraine had three children. How would we talk to them? Would we need to find Lorraine's dead body in a ditch to give her a proper burial? Then, there were our families to reunite with. As we expected, dealing with people who thought you were dead was both depressing and rejuvenating.

Then there were the legal matters. Knowing that Paul would distort the truth, I used my free time on the barge to write my own account on the crash of the S-440. Although this project was meant to be a coping mechanism, most of the book was presented as evidence in court. Lucas contributed his own commentary on the circumstances surrounding the crash.

When he gained the strength, Lucas liked to walk along the metal scraps to find something interesting. He didn't hesitate to tell me long-winded stories about how special the technology used to be to him. "This was a platform they used to teach typing in school" or "this was how we used to watch movies," he would reminisce. Most of the items he pointed out to me didn't work and would be thrown right back into the trash.

After pleading with Lucas to show the Ogedei forgiveness, he presented a pleasant side of himselfthat allowed him to get along with the rest of the men just fine (a slight annoyance for me). This was all thanks to the boisterous nights the crew hosted with their card game called *Mai*, which Lucas excelled at because it reminded him of poker. In the last four days of our sail, I beat Jerimiem and eventually became the resident queen at *Mai*.

Although the port for New Khan was far from the actual city, New Khan was unmistakable. The bright neon commercials, the ripping of motor engines, the horns of trains, the carbon copy skyscrapers pasted one after the other were hard to miss and overwhelming. My head hurt from the overwhelming bleach smell. Time spun five times faster in New Khan, which didn't feel right to me.

On the morning before we docked back at the city, I was sweeping the deck when I saw a strange woman with excessively shiny gray hair. I was genuinely confused because I knew the barge inside out, and I was the only woman on board.

"Excuse me?" I asked her. She turned around and looked at me with a pale, powdered face. "Who are you?" I asked.

The woman smiled and showed a familiar poorly powdered red nose that reminded me of Captain Yank's. "Hellooo my dearrr." Captain Yank giggled in a fake high-pitched voice. "You like my face?" he asked me. I inspected it more closely.

"That's a well-made mask. Is it really one? Even your facial expressions are reflected in your mask," I said. Captain Yank laughed.

"This mask was expensive, but it hides me well from recognition cameras," he said, then raised his voice's pitch. "All the businessmen know to buy goodies from Aunty Yanny."

At last, the barge docked at the port. I thanked the crew excessively for their generosity in my broken Ogedei language. I thanked Baine for her guidance. She bowed her head and handed me my light crossbow.

"Practice," she said, winking at me.

I thanked Jerimiem for taking my side and sympathizing with me. I thanked Shering for the meals he prepared. I thanked Captain Yank for his upbeat energy. And finally, I turned to Z.

"Thank you for saving me," I told Z. "And for your patience and mentorship. I wouldn't be here, on Earth, if it weren't for you."

"You are daughter to us." He told me, raising his dark spectacles for once to show his dark eyes. "You looked like you can't do anything, but you have one crazy beast inside you." I still wanted to convey the genuine respect that I had for this man, but I couldn't quite fit in all that I wanted to say.

"I'll be back," I told him while shaking his hand. "Would you let me back in? I want to work under you. I want to help G and her prosthetics."

Z shrugged. "We will see."

Lucas and I were the first living load to be dropped off the barge in a long time. Captain Yank was in his all-female form at the rudder, waving his sweat-stained sailor hat to me. The barge sailed away with its load of electric stoves, military tanks, yellowing telephones, flat screen TVs, and harvested metal valuables to the auction sale.

On unsteady legs, we landed back to where it had begun. Would we be happier back in NK City? Would we be accepted back into our families? How would we emotionally deal with Lorraine's death? Would our crazy stories be believed in court? I didn't know the answers to those questions, but I knew that life in NK City would never be the same.

EPILOGUE

Dear G,

I thought I saw the faint outline of Jerimiem's scar through his disguise near the port, which I like to traverse on my morning walks. He told me that he was spending time with his *lady* and asked that I *please* refer to him as Ronnie. I got a chance to talk to him in private and he said he would pass on this letter to you. Here is my shot at reconnecting with you and imparting what I want you to know the most. Hope this letter doesn't get lost. . . .

Today marks a year since the crash. It's weird to celebrate unfortunate events, but if you recall my rescued crewmate Lucas and I gathered together to commemorate Lorraine's death. We have a lot of feelings, but they boil down to this: it's been a crazy year and our lives are far from normal. That's not a bad thing. I really am grateful to be alive.

You and Z were right. I came back and was surprised at how disillusioned I felt. I used to stay in and entertain myself with Cort, the equivalent of a friend. When I was sad, I would easily fall into the trap of constantly cycling from one medium to the other. I would try to fulfill my needs and fill my time with passivity. Now, I wish I could back to Ogedei and see how happy Nia is with her sister or come back to play with My-Ra. The children in your settlement surprised me; I used to have their same level of excitement to be an adult. And now, that has all evaporated.

Every single day since coming back, I have felt paralyzed by how little decisions were made beyond me. I am bombarded with information to make me think one way or the next. It's easier to shut down and sleep away. I have constant headaches.

When I lived with you and Z, I finally felt like I had returned to the familiar feeling of comfort. It reminded me of when my mom created that protective coat of warmth around me. She was encouraging, criticizing, helping, advising, but all out of love.

Since my mother's passing, I have been a meandering adult, trying to survive and work.

I'm not good with words, but it was such a relief to be part of your family with you, Z, and even My-Ra. Over these past years, I was so caught up in taking care of people around me, such as my mother, that I became drained. I lost sight of what I wanted for myself. Thank you for taking care of me and filling my cup.

The results from the trial came back. I stopped caring about what would happen to the company or Paul or anyone else. Constantly reliving the crash or the death of my crewmate Lorraine was tiring. I realized I had only lived on my own for three days, but that time period felt like eternity.

Lucas and I won the lawsuit and split the money. He was ecstatic and immediately declared himself a retired, free man. And the money is truly enough to support me for a long time, possibly through retirement.

Lucas and I are close friends now. His wife sometimes has a difficult time understanding the circumstances of our crash and at one point even accused Lucas of cheating with me, not understanding that Lucas and I share a bond that's far from sexual. She's still a sweetheart and eventually understood, although she constantly tries to push her twice-divorced younger son, Aiden, onto me. I wish that I could tell you about him—see what you think. We are only acquaintances, but his divorce rate is far from attractive.

I've been looking to use my money to buy professional-grade prosthetics for your hands. The ones I've been eyeing provide astute fine motorcontrol skills. They would be perfect for you to learn to play the guitar the proper way! I'm hoping I'll be able to send them to you.

This is all to say that I would love to come back home to live in Ogedei. I thought I felt a connection to New Khan, but I don't anymore. This city depresses me. There's nothing to do except click on a button like a caged mouse.

I know your reservations about my coming back to society as that will endanger Z. I promise you that these are far from my intentions and Z has my utmost respect.

I hope that you trust me enough to let me back into your lives and pay you back for saving me.

Please let Z know that he was a fantastic trainer, and working with him was an honor. Hope that My-Ra is doing well.

Hope to hear from you someday,

A

ACKNOWLEDGMENTS

There is no doubt in my mind that *Air Unplugged* would have stayed as a collection of Google Drive folders and never come to existence without the support of a team of people, whether named here explicitly or not.

Thank you to my beta readers, Apurva Shrestha and Joshua Gibson, who helped steer the novel in the right direction. Your feedback was exactly what I needed to hear to make critical plot decisions. Thank you so much for your timely feedback.

Thank you to the people who made this personal project financially possible! I was overwhelmed by the financial support I received, as well as by those who spread the word regarding my campaign efforts:

Jackie Garraffa	Ajitha Bala
Danielle Dilgard	Jessica Taylor
Kabita Pradhan	Ryan Keough
Kajal Shrestha	Andrew Kidd
Kritika Shrestha	Rawan Osman
Carolyn Skowron	Sharon Gravatt
Ethan Schlussel	Mae Layne
Bracken Carter	Melinda Harden
Sampurna Maharjan	Rachael CB Osborne
Sushil Lal Shrestha	Cori Bider

Jad Abutayeh
Raven Witherspoon
Chideraa Ekechukwu
Devin Esleck
Rebecca Whitten
Abby Sebold
Kirill Shalakov
Yelena S Kim
Caitlin Phan
Lindsey Norberg
Vibha Patil
Geneva Lanzetta
Emily Duong
Ethan Rozario
Cady Rombach
Autumn Baker
Konnov Andrey
Tiffany Nguyen
Elizabeth and Jason
Joshua Sukhdeo
Ajay Mathew
Yolanda Yao
Kathryn Nerys Apple
Megan Lee
Jordan Young
Robert Shafer
Devin Pendse
Dylan Miks
Yong Yu Khristy Zheng
Conner Childs
Jacob Gibson

Dan-Thanh Dang
Erin Klich
Jackie Claure Lapidus
Olivia BeVier
Librado Anglero
Lee Knapp
Megan Sundberg
Marina Avetisyan
Brianna Guest
Abbie Morgan
Miriam Mindel
Jefferson Pan
Jenna Hofrichter
Eric Koester
Ana Tsiskarishvili
Kenneth and Margaret Brown
Drew Tada
James Weeden
Charlie Cuccherini
Margarita T
Svetlana Eroshenko
Conner Hauck
Sara Blackburn
Collin James Shumaker
Jacob Wasinger
Joshua O'Neill Gibson
Apurva Lal Shrestha
Lena P
Derek Wu
Camille Do
Konstantin Akopiants

Thank you to my editors—Camryn Privette, Mozelle Jordan, and Karina Agbisit—who bore with me, my emotional roller coasters, and my crunch time writing. Thank you Stephen D. Howard for mentoring me and for the constant fountain of ideas. Thank you to New Degree Press for providing me with the motivation and resources to be able to create, and thank you to Eric Koester for taking the time to listen to my idea about a helicopter crash with a feminine protagonist.

Dare I say it, I'm also thankful for the events that inspired this book. Although my original inspiration for *Air Unplugged* was traumatic, writing those feelings and growing past them through this book was such a relief.

And finally, I'm so thankful for the support I received from my family and friends when writing the book. I wasn't expecting anyone to care, but the overwhelming response was a pleasant surprise. Thank you to all my friends who listened to me stress and ramble about writing. Thank you all.

www.ingramcontent.com/pod-product-compliance
Lightning Source LLC
Chambersburg PA
CBHW051455050726
47593CB00005B/2081